WHY NOT ME?

THE KEYS TO UNLOCK YOUR POWER
AND RELEASE YOUR POTENTIAL

*Be kind to yourself & good
people will find you.*

MARK E. MEINCKE

Cover design by Define Curious Design
www.definecurious.com

ISBN-10: 1533367043
ISBN-13: 978-1533367044

First Edition: October 2008
Second Edition: May 2016

Visit www.amazon.com for additional copies

Printed in the USA

TABLE OF CONTENTS

CHAPTER 3
THE TOOLS TO REALIZE
YOUR PURPOSE

CHAPTER 4
MOVING BEYOND MEDIOCRE

CHAPTER 5
THE WISDOM TO
MAXIMIZE YOUR POTENTIAL

CONCLUSION

ABOUT THE AUTHOR

Advanced Praise for "*Why Not Me?*"

Why Not Me inspires, encourages and motivates beyond expectations. A truly enjoyable read.

—*Captain Troy Dumka, Air Canada Pilot*

Why Not Me is an inspiring book that entertains, enlightens and Empowers.

—*Meretta Pater, Award Winning Novelist*

Why Not Me is packed with valuable tools which enable the reader to be successful and fulfilled.

—*Wayne Lee, Author, Speaker, Entertainer*

Comprehensive, compelling and completely thorough. For those wishing to realize their full potential, Mr. Meincke's book contains a wealth of wisdom and tools to elevate both life, and business.

—*David Donnelly, Contributing Author to the New York Times Best Selling, Masters of Sales*

INTRODUCTION

The keys I've decided to share with you are not the only keys that are of value. There are many more; however, you will find those other keys as a natural result of using the ones I have provided in this book. I didn't want to overload you with information, so I only shared these primary keys that will lead you to any of the further keys you may require or find useful.

In a way, this book is my autobiography. The lessons I am sharing are the same lessons I needed to learn to turn my own life around. I wasn't born with a silver spoon in my mouth, nor did I have access to the understanding of my own abilities or resources. All I had was a burning feeling deep down that told me I was capable of far more than the evidence seemed to indicate. Resumes are used as evidence of your capabilities, and my resume wouldn't have impressed anyone in my early years. Resumes can't show what you are capable of or what your true purpose in life is. Somehow, I had a knowledge of myself that was beyond my resume, and it is this knowledge that gave me the strength to move forward and to grow.

Throughout grade school, I was always placed in the "special education" classes. I just didn't fit in the school system, so they didn't know what else to do with me. All of the tests they threw at me indicated that I was unusually bright, yet there I was with the "challenged" kids. In my early years, I was told that I was a "slow learner." Once I accepted that misplaced label, I gave up at school. There didn't seem to be a point in trying, so instead, I decided to scrape by with as little effort as possible. As a result of my decision to be a problem student, I failed both grade four and grade nine. I didn't even graduate high school until I was twenty years old. This fact used to be way too embarrassing for me to admit. Today, instead of being embarrassed, I'm actually quite proud of myself for refusing to be a quitter and not dropping out of high school. It was very uncomfortable for me to be one of only two people out of 1,200 who were twenty years old in Grade Twelve. I just decided that being a twenty-year-old in high school wasn't as embarrassing as being a drop out. That one simple decision was the fuel I needed to keep going.

To pull myself out of this hole of low self worth, I had to learn the lessons that are shared in this book. These tools, or keys, are fully transferable. Once acquired, you will be able to pass them onto those who ask you to share them. I hope that you are generous with this information, as it is needed badly by people from all walks of life. Just remember that you can only help people who are asking for help.

I am eternally thankful for the teachings of my friends and family. There are people in my life who were able to see my potential long before I could see it in myself, and there are people who still cannot see it to this day. I'm grateful to the people on both sides of this fence, as they all have contributed to my success, either directly or indirectly. Everyone has lessons to teach if you have learned how to listen.

I have a handful of friends who stood by me at a time when I felt unworthy of the company of good people. I'm not sure I would have stood by the person who I used to be, but they did. Somehow, they were able to look past my resume and see my potential. It's a truly gifted person who has this ability, and I am incredibly blessed to have them in my inner circle.

Some of the keys I am sharing with you will assist you to see past other people's resumes as well as your own. With this X-ray vision, you will be able to see through the negative shell that many have to the positive core that is trying to burst out of most of us.

This book has been arranged to provide a cumulative impact. Each key is intended to set the foundation to learn the next keys to follow. I have endeavored to make this book far more than just a text of valuable information; I wish for you to absorb the positive lessons in this book in a meaningful and useful way. My intention is not just to sell millions of copies of this book, but to create the largest positive impact I can.

Another key feature of this book is that it is designed to also be used as a quick reference guide. I've often tried to review a particular lesson from a book, but I couldn't remember in which chapter it was buried. To alleviate this frustration, I've broken this book down into a unique format of individual keys. Each key contains information that has been placed in **bold** font. The parts in bold are often key phrases or quotes that are intended to encapsulate the essence of each key.

The extensive use of quotes in this book is intended to provide greater depth of understanding for each key. By providing quotes, I'm providing alternate ways to phrase a particular thought. By seeing a concept through many different sets of eyes, you are more likely to find a style that works for you and thus maximize the depth of your understanding of that concept.

I wish you well, and thank you for allowing me to join you for the next few steps of your journey toward releasing your potential.

CHAPTER 1
UNLOCKING YOUR POWER

KEY #1
FAITH IN YOURSELF

Faith in yourself is the foundation required upon which to build anything you wish for your life. Once you truly believe in the fact that you not only have the ability to create any life you wish for yourself but that you deserve to have that life, then you will have started on the road to getting what you want.

Believing you can achieve is different from believing that you are worthy of an achievement. It's one thing to recognize your own talent and another to believe you deserve to benefit from your talents. Without the sense of self-worth that speaks to you saying "**you deserve** to achieve anything you set your sights on," you'll never take aim at the things you wish to do with your life.

All people have self-limiting beliefs. The challenge is to realize that these beliefs are self-imposed; therefore, they can be self-removed. With the understanding that we get in our own way and with the faith in our ability to remove our self-imposed obstacles, we will then have the required foundation upon which we can stack up new skills, abilities, and knowledge. We must come to the point where we realize that, if others can achieve a particular goal, then **"Why not me?"**

Let's boil this down.

You must have faith that:

- The information in this book can give you access to the tools required to accomplish any goal you choose to set for yourself.

- You have the ability to learn the skills and develop the abilities necessary to get what you want.

- It is your God-given right to have the opportunity to be emotionally healthy, happy, and financially secure.

- You deserve the opportunity to be emotionally healthy, happy, and financially secure.

- There is no reason at all for you to not have what you desire most.

- What you want is 100% attainable.

For your faith to grow, you must grow. Read and strive to understand the lessons in this book, and your faith in your ability and potential will build. Within these pages lies the wisdom required to put you in a healthy frame of mind. If you don't have a successful mindset, you can't be successful to any great degree. You must learn the difference between an enabling belief and a disabling belief so you can identify the thought habits that may be keeping your dreams from coming true. You must also identify the thought habits that keep you from dreaming at all.

This book is full of both famous and original quotations that have powerful significance. If you read nothing else here, read everything that is in **bold** and you will grow at least a little. Each time you read this book, different messages will hit you and stick with you. It's impossible to absorb all of this information in its entirety when first being introduced to the concepts. New concepts take time to sink in, so be patient and exert the effort to re-read this book many times over. You should also read many other books like this one as well. If you have trouble chewing through an entire book, don't worry about it. This book is designed to double as a quick reference guide as well. If there is a particular topic that you wish to delve into, just choose the key that you wish to review from the index, and away you go. This book can be thought of as the *Yellow Pages*™ for success. It is best that you read it all, but if you just aren't the type of person who can read an entire book, at least there will still be some value here for you.

Each lesson learned will open new doors to understanding further lessons, and so on. Just because you are familiar with an idea, doesn't mean that you have a full understanding of it. **Ideas have layers.** On the surface, you may recognize an idea. But as you peel off the layers and get to the core of an idea, you will find that your understanding will grow and deepen. The deeper your understanding is of a concept, the more useful it is to you. Even though I'm writing this book, my own understanding of its lessons continually get deeper and more meaningful as I read the same concepts written by other authors from other perspectives. I'm considered by many to be an expert on successful thinking; however, I only consider myself to be an apt pupil. There is always more to learn.

> *The student strives to be the master, and the master realizes that he will always be a student.*
>
> *Chinese proverb*

KEY # 2
OWNERSHIP

Our lives all start out more or less the same, as a blank slate. Some people have greater challenges than others; some have better resources such as good parents or role-models from whom they can learn. Country or origin is certainly a factor, since there are more challenges in a poor country than a wealthy one (but not less opportunity). Regardless of circumstance, our lives all start out the same—a bright light, a smack on the bum, and a sudden gasp that is our first breath.

Regardless of the relatively even starting line, we have successful people and unsuccessful people. We have people who had a terrible childhood, full of violence, pain, poverty, and low self-esteem, yet they end up living happy and fulfilling lives. We find privileged children with every economic and social advantage who end up as drug addicts and/or criminals and lead empty lives. The tabloids and entertainment channels are loaded with stories every week that prove this to be true. How is it that modern-day famous divas can end up in jail for drugs or drunk driving? How do multi-million-dollar movie super stars end up in jail for tax evasion? At the other end of the scale, how does a welfare mom end up as a billionaire author such as JK Rowling? How does a sexually abused, dirt poor, African American woman become one of the most influential people on the planet, such as Oprah Winfrey?

It stands to reason that the components of both success and failure can be identified and therefore duplicated for our benefit. It also stands to reason that it isn't your parents or the neighborhood you grew up in that determines your success in life.

When things go wrong or our lives fail to meet our expectations, it's natural to try to find someone to blame. The last person we want to point fingers at is ourselves. I've found that laying blame does nothing more than validate excuses and allow the unfortunate to fall into the "victim rut." If the keys to success and failure aren't the influential people who helped mold us into adults, then what are they? What makes some people succeed in living a happy life and others condemned to a life devoid of accomplishments and validation?

The most successful people on earth all agree that **the keys to getting what you want have nothing to do with the world**

**around you. Instead, success has everything to do with
the world within you. It is your internal circumstances,
not your external ones that determine what shape your
life will take.** Once you have taken ownership of this fact,
thus ownership of your own life, the whole world will look
different to you. You will see opportunities where you once
saw obstacles, and you will see the good in situations where
you used to see only the bad. **Ownership of your life is a
critical key for you to accept and obtain.**

The intention of this book is to provide you with access to a
full ring of keys that can unlock the doors that are currently
locked tight. Some of these keys or tools you already have,
and others may be foreign to you. For the keys that you
already have, you will be able to polish off any rust that
may exist. For the keys that you've never before considered
owning, I hope that you enjoy having your shiny new keys
jingle on your keychain. Once you have acquired a key, it
can never be taken from you. They can and will get rusty if
you don't look after them, but you will never lose them.

> *"The mind, once expanded, can never
> return to its original size."*
> *Oliver Wendell Holmes*

It is your field and your barn

Think of your life as a farmer's field, with good topsoil and
ample irrigation. We all own our own field (our own life),
and we all have the same basic opportunity. However, good
dirt isn't enough to grow a good healthy crop! I think we

can all agree that we need equipment, fertilizer, and fuel for the equipment. Of course, we also need some way to learn how to use, repair, and maintain the equipment. Once we have all of this figured out and we have a good crop, we then have to acquire more equipment and skills to operate the machinery so that we can harvest our crop.

We're not finished yet. We have done all of this work and still haven't made a dime! We still need to acquire a grain bin to store our harvest and augers to move it from the combine to the grain bin and from the grain bin to the transport truck. Now we need to find the best place to sell our crop and decide on the best time to sell it to achieve maximum profit.

So, what's my point? What does this have to do with you? Let's go back to the beginning.

Your life is a fertile field; all of the equipment and knowledge required to get a bountiful harvest is within your grasp. Imagine a huge barn, the biggest barn that you've ever seen. In this barn is all of the equipment and knowledge required to harvest any crop you plant. You own this barn and its contents. It is yours, and nobody can take it from you. Now here's the trick: it's locked tight. Not even a safecracker or locksmith can open this lock. Nobody can open the lock for you. But you can open it any time you wish, because **you have access to the keys!** If you choose to learn how to claim your field and your barn as your own, then this book will supply you with access to your keys. Once you have the keys, it will be up to you to unlock the door, open it, learn how to operate the equipment, and decide to **use your newfound resources** to achieve your goals. Think of each key as a learnable skill. Each new skill you acquire will accelerate your life in any direction you choose. The more skills you have, the faster your life will move toward your chosen direction.

Let us paraphrase this thought:

> **Your life is an enormous field, and <u>you own this field</u>. On this field is a huge barn filled with all the tools you need to turn your field into whatever you wish it to be. <u>You own this barn</u> and its contents.**

Once you realize you already own your own life and you are in control of the direction your life is headed, it is up to you to accept the responsibility for the results. Only you can plant the seeds and reap the harvest. No one can do this for you. The concept of ownership is a scary one and requires courage to accept. The bigger you wish your life to be, the bigger the responsibility you must be able to accept. **First comes the courage to accept responsibility for the result of your actions, and then comes the confidence in your ability to create positive results.** If you are waiting for the confidence to come first, you are putting the cart before the horse. Confidence comes from seeing the positive results you have created, so you can't have results until you have taken action. Courage is what allows you to take any action you have never taken before.

If all of this sounds like a lot of work, you're right, it is. That's farming, and that's life. If you want to get anything out of your life, you have to suck it up and do the work. Success may be difficult, **but it is attainable!**

> *"Failure happens consistently to those who refuse to do what successful people insist on doing."*
>
> **unknown**

Ponder this, it's a key rule. Read it over again and again. Keep this in your mind. It is so very important for you to acknowledge this simple truth.

> *"If you do only what you need to do to get by, then get by you will. But the end results will not be outstanding or exceptional. You have to do what others don't want to do to have an edge."*
>
> **Donald Trump**

Getting what you want isn't easy, but it is simple. One thing is for certain: finding the keys to that barn of yours will take **hard work, faith, and an open mind.** If you're not ready to learn, then you won't finish this book or any other similar book. However, if you do finish this book and embark on a healthy journey to a more successful life, the **hard work** required won't feel like hard work at all. Once you adjust your perspective, you will look forward to and enjoy the work ahead.

Hard work is a fact of life. Laziness is a fact of failure, but here is the good news. The keys to opening the barn and releasing your potential are within your grasp! Your creator wants you to claim what is rightfully yours, but you have to do the work. Here's how:

1. Believe that you own the keys, the barn, and all of its contents.

2. Be willing to learn how to find the keys

3. Have faith that you deserve the keys, the barn, and all the contents.

4. Be willing to do the work to plant, harvest, and sell your crop.

If I still have your attention, then I suggest that you re-read keys #1 & #2 before you continue any further. I'm asking for your "**hard work, faith, and an open mind.**" What you have read so far creates the foundation for all of the other keys. The stronger that foundation is, the stronger your understanding will be of all the next keys.

KEY #3
PARADIGM

If you are to adjust your way of thinking, you must first understand why it is you think as you do. We are all governed by paradigms. A paradigm is a set of rules that governs how you view the world around you. Have you ever heard of "thinking outside the box"? The box is your own personal paradigm. The walls of this box can be very difficult to move, depending on how rigid your belief system is. The more rigid you are, the less you will be able to adjust your mind-set. It is the fear of change that keeps us rigid. **The only way to have something that you've never had is to do something that you have never done**...so if you want something, you're going to have to change. With increased confidence, you will find that adjusting your thinking doesn't have to be scary. The more you learn, the more your confidence will grow.

All people have self-made walls in their minds that limit their potential (paradigms). Successful people have simply learned how to take down most of the walls hindering their success, whereas most other people leave the walls standing. These walls keep our potential and our success at bay. Understanding that it is **you** who is holding yourself back, not your spouse, the job market, your boss, your parents, or any other external influence, is a huge accomplishment. If you give yourself permission to succeed and allow abundance to flow into your life, it will. You just have to remove the self-imposed barriers that we all have. **With each self-imposed obstacle removed, your life will move forward at an ever-increasing rate of speed.**

> *"Definition of insanity: To keep doing the same thing over and over again, then expect a different result."*
>
> *Albert Einstein*

KEY# 4
BE A STUDENT

"Empty the coins of your purse into your mind, and your mind will fill your purse with coins."

Ben Franklin

If this is the first book you've read on personal development, I sure hope it won't be your last. It doesn't matter how much you know. If you stop learning, you stop living a rich and meaningful life. According to author Stephen R. Covey, the seventh habit of highly successful people is to read "personal development" books constantly. The thing about "*THE TRUTH*" is that there is only one truth. There are different ways to express it, and this book is simply "*the truth*" channeled through the "Mark Meincke" filter. This book is designed to share wisdom with you in a way that has as much of an impact as possible. Every detail of this book is designed to maximize your ability to absorb the wisdom within; however, reading other related books will still increase the depth of your understanding.

It's critically important to continually sharpen your axe and to add new tools to the tool box. Here is a Canadian version of the story that Stephen R. Covey shares in his book, *The Seven Habits of Highly Successful People* :

> Two lumberjacks were left in the finals of the Yukon's annual lumberjack competition. One man was the reigning champion for three years running. He was

a huge brute of a man who possessed such a ridiculous strength that none had been able to challenge him till this day.

The challenger wasn't a small man, but still he was only half the size of the champion lumberjack. When the final competition was able to get under way, the challenger looked calm as he simply sharpened his axe with great care.

The competition was to see who could chop through twenty logs the fastest. It was a grueling task that took enormous skill, power, and endurance. Few men would be able to even complete such a task in a single day.

When the bell rang, the two brutes sprang into action and started chopping feverously. After the first log, the challenger stopped, pulled his sharpening stone out of his pocket, and carefully re-honed the edge. The crowd roared with laughter, and the champion grinned wide with confidence. There was no way that this challenger could win if he wasted time sharpening his axe after every log!

After a few moments of sharpening, the challenger confidently went on to the next log. Once through, he repeated the task of sharpening his axe. After every single log, the challenger never failed to stick to his routine. As champion finished chopping through his seventeenth log, he was surprised to notice the challenger was at his eighteenth log! Suddenly realizing the importance of a sharp axe, the champ started working on his dull axe, but it was too late. The champion's axe was way too dull and pitted to be brought back to a fine edge any time soon.

The challenger won by two logs.

> **Growth is a habit worth developing. If you start the habit of learning from your mistakes and seeking out wisdom, growth will soon become a healthy addiction.**

Quotes on Be a Student:

> *"The book you don't read won't help."*
>
> **Jim Rohn**

> *"The soft-minded man always fears change. He feels security in the status quo, and he has an almost morbid fear of the new. For him, the greatest pain is the pain of a new idea."*
>
> **Rev. Dr. Martin Luther King, Jr.**

> *"Fear can only prevail when victims are ignorant of the facts."*
>
> **Thomas Jefferson**

"Man's mind stretched to a new idea never goes back to its original dimensions"

Oliver Wendell Holmes

"Learning is a treasure that will follow its owner everywhere."

Chinese Proverb

"There are three kinds of men:
Some learn by reading.
A few learn by observation.
The rest of them have to pee on the electric fence."

Will Rogers

"The man who doesn't read good books has no advantage over the man who can't read them."

Mark Twain

The more you grow as a person, the more you will achieve in both your personal and professional life.

You have to grow old, but you don't have to grow up. Sadly, it's all too common for people to stop growing, learning, and maturing at a young age, yet live to a ripe old age.

KEY # 5
THE POWER OF PERSPECTIVE

To get what you want, you first have to see it clearly.

Success is a journey, not a destination. The keys can only be achieved by walking a path. I can only provide access, and only you can walk towards the keys. Walking towards the keys takes **hard work, faith, and an open mind**.

Understanding the **power of perspective** is one of the most important keys you can acquire. The "maze" metaphor will help to provide an understanding of the power of perspective.

The "Maze" Metaphor

Have you ever seen one of those huge mazes that are made out of a corn field? They can be absolutely massive. Even with a map, they can take hours to navigate.

Imagine being totally lost in a big maze. If only you had someone in a balloon above the maze who could clearly see all of the trails and dead ends so that he could guide you. With a little guidance, you wouldn't be running into so many frustrating dead ends. Think of the principles within this book as tools that can assist you to see new opportunities purely because of perspective. You can bumble through the maze on your own, or you can accept help and navigate the maze much more effectively. Think of the relief you would feel if you weren't running into dead ends all of the time.

The guide in the balloon above **is not** smarter than you. If you were in a balloon above the maze, you could see the same thing as the guide! Once you get out of the maze, you will have your own balloon (it's in your barn) so that you can help others navigate as well.

For a practical example of the maze metaphor, just think about the last time you were on the phone, trying to give directions to a friend so he could get to your home for the first time. In your mind, you can see the "bird's-eye view" of your neighborhood as if you were up in a balloon looking down on the streets, with a clear view of the correct path. Do you remember what it was like trying to convey the directions to your friend? Did you feel that your friend was a big dummy for not knowing how to get to your home? Of course not! Until the directions were given, how could anyone find your home? Once your friend has made the journey a few times, he will be able to picture your home from a bird's-eye view as well, and then he will be able to pass on the directions to others.

Everyone is looking for the same trails that get us to the same destination. Everyone wants to feel respected, loved, important, satisfied, and just plain happy. We are all in our own personal maze, trying to get through life the best we can. Those of us with balloons have the perspective to get through the maze much easier and with far more success. We all have access to a balloon of our own. We just have to realize it and take action to use it.

So, as you can see, **it is not brain power that has people taking the easy path through life; it is perspective, or point of view.** Have you ever had one of those "ah-ha" moments? That moment where you say, "Oh! I get it now. I never looked at it like that before. Now it makes perfect sense." You had a shift in perspective. What was once hidden suddenly became perfectly clear by simply adjusting your point of view. It's like bringing binoculars into focus; with a slight adjustment, the blurry becomes clear. If you refuse to adjust the focus, of course you will never be able to see clearly.

Early in my success, one of my closest friends asked me how I was doing in my professional life. I knew there wasn't huge amount of money to show, yet, but I also knew that I was on the right path to a healthy income. So I answered honestly, "Business is awesome! I'm achieving all my financial goals ahead of schedule, and I couldn't be happier." Now this was true, but for him to understand this, he would have to already have the same tools I had that got me to this point in my life. Sadly, he hadn't found the key to his own barn yet, so he was quite skeptical about my success. I showed him my records with my second year income on it. It was fairly large, and it was more than double the gross income of my first year. Doubling your income in a year is a huge accomplishment for any business owner but he wasn't very impressed at all.

Although I was proud of my accomplishment and excited about the year ahead, my good friend told me what I had just achieved was no big deal and I was deluded if I believed that I was successful. He wasn't trying to be mean; **he just didn't have the perspective to accurately see my business for what it was.** He was in the maze, bumping into dead ends, and I was above in the balloon watching him, wishing I could help.

Now, many people would have been so upset with a good friend telling them their dreams were pie–in-the-sky that they might have given up or been deterred. Luckily, I was confident that my friend's negative remarks were just a product of a limited perspective. As it turned out, I was validated by **tripling** my second year's income in my third year.

I'm sharing this because, although I was not deterred by my friend, I was initially upset by his words. Despite my display of confidence, I still fought nagging doubts about my own ability. The last thing I needed was to be discouraged by a close friend. Fortunately for me, I had the right tools. I was able to ignore both my friend's doubts as well as my own, and carry on. I used his doubt as a motivator to do well and to show him just how wrong his negative thinking was. It may not have been the healthiest motivator, but it did work.

Today, it would be impossible for me to be hurt by a friend's negative words. Through perspective, I now understand that the negative comments aimed at me have nothing to do with me. When someone attacks you, they are revealing weaknesses or fears in themselves. If you are doing something wonderful with your life and they feel that their own life is not wonderful, they will downplay your success so that they don't have to feel surpassed. Sadly, it's very common for our own family members to be the ones who downplay and trivialize our success. As my wife has often said, "Family is the first to see you fail." Of course, this isn't true in every family, but it is very common. **Negative words have the potential to hurt the most when they're from those closest to us**. This is why it's so important to be able to distance yourself from the harmful words of others.

> *"Every obnoxious act is a cry for help."*
> *Zig Ziglar*

> *"Few things are harder to put up with*
> *than the annoyance of a good example."*
> *Mark Twain*

KEY #6
THE PERSPECTIVE OF NEGATIVE PEOPLE

A negative comment from an adult shouldn't sound any different to you than a negative comment from a young child. If a four-year-old comes up to you and says, "You're stupid," although you may find this rude, you certainly wouldn't walk away wondering if that kid was right. You are mature enough to consider the source, and because you realize that the kid just doesn't know any better, you brush it off. When an adult insults you, it's exactly the same; they just don't know any better. When the insult is from someone who you love and respect, the same principal applies. By mastering this one perspective, you'll release yourself from much resentment and anger. See each insult as if it has come from the lips of a young child who is having a temper tantrum. By seeing the negative person for who they are, you will be able to replace an angry reaction with one of understanding and even pity.

> *"Resentment is like drinking poison,*
> *then waiting for the other person to die."*
> *Carrie Fisher*

Expecting a negative person to care about your feelings, is like expecting a man to give birth; he just doesn't have the right tools for the job.

KEY# 7
PERSPECTIVE OF FAILURE

It is absolutely critical that you are conscious of how you view failure. **Failure is a fact of life and a key ingredient to success.** How you view failure is a critical skill that you **must** acquire to find the keys to your barn.

Here is a portrait of an achiever that you might find interesting.

- 1832 Failed in business; bankruptcy

- 1832 Defeated for legislature

- 1834 Failed in business again; bankruptcy

- 1835 Fiancée died

- 1836 Nervous breakdown

- 1838 Again defeated in another election

- 1843 Defeated for US Congress

- 1848 Defeated for US Congress again!

- 1855 Defeated for US Senate

- 1856 Defeated for Vice President of the United States

- 1858 Defeated again for the Senate

Most people would have given up by now, but not this guy. Wait for it—

- 1860 Elected President of the United States!

This man was Abraham Lincoln. This is a fine example of the fact that **you can not fail unless you quit.** If President Lincoln ever lost his positive attitude and internalized his multiple failures, he would have never carried on in his political pursuit. **He was never afraid of failing, only of quitting.** His life story is also proof that **your future does not have to be a slave to your past.**

Have you ever heard of Sir Winston Churchill? His history was a lot like Lincoln's. Churchill had a political resume that was full of failures and missteps. Today, he's remembered as one of the greatest world leaders in modern history. There are even political science courses dedicated to just him and his great success as a Prime Minister of Great Britain.

Churchill's multiple past failures were all due to the fact that he was a square peg trying to fit into a round hole. His destiny was to be the Prime Minister, and any other function was not a proper fit for him. Once he was in a position that suited him, he excelled as an amazing leader.

If these great men allowed themselves to view each challenge and setback in their lives as "personal failures," they never would have had the strength to continue. When most people fail, they internalize the failure and feel that the failed attempt means that *they* are failures. As a result, people suffer unnecessarily from low self-esteem and a lack of confidence. **Successful people realize that there is no such thing as failure; there are only desirable and undesirable results.**

I've read the Lincoln example above in many different success books, and I fear that someone with the stature of Lincoln or Churchill might be a bit tough to relate to. So, let me share another, more personal, example, from a different angle.

My own search wasn't for political office, but only for a fulfilling life. I wanted a life that allowed my skills to shine; one that satisfied me. I traveled many different paths on this search, the first of which was when I joined the Army at the age of twenty. I knew I wasn't a text book "Army Guy," but I also somehow knew that I needed a path, and **any good path was better than no path at all.**

I had barely scraped through high school with a vocational diploma, and I had no idea what I wanted to do with my life. All I knew was that if I dove into the three-year commitment of the military I would be a better man at the end of that path than taking no path at all. I knew that the world would at least see me as a man of some courage who could finish what he starts. Serving coffee at the local donut shop wasn't going to provide that for me. I didn't know where this path would lead, only that it would lead to a better place than the donut shop. I made the leap of faith, joined the Army, and went beyond my three-year commitment to do a total of five years. I not only finished what I started, I stayed on a little more so that I could accomplish more goals within the Army. I wanted to do a UN Peace Keeping tour of Croatia, so I signed on for longer than my initial commitment.

This path was not the right path for me, nor was the next one, or the next seven paths after that. However, instead of feeling lost, I knew that none of the wrong paths were a waste of my time. Each path I traveled provided me with new skills and new lessons about life and about myself.

Regardless of the frustration of walking so many of the wrong paths, something deep inside me wouldn't allow me to feel discouraged even though I was quite mediocre at most of the paths that I had tried thus far. **I knew I had talents; I just wasn't sure what they were or how to express them**. Every negative experience, every failed attempt, was a lesson that taught me how **NOT** to live my life! It was only with this knowledge, and by the elimination of other paths, that I was able to get on the path I am on now. If I had ever adopted the **victim** mindset, and said, "Why do I suck at everything I try? Why won't life just give me a break and let me be happy?"—if I had ever popped my thumb into my mouth and let myself topple over into that "Victim Rut"—then I never would have grown; I never would had been able to have the amazing life that I now enjoy.

I was mediocre at the other paths, because they were not the right paths. Once I had realized my own strengths and accepted my weaknesses, I was then able to choose a path that was appropriate for me. Just because you don't have a talent for math, doesn't mean you don't have a talent for football. We all have our talents; it's just a matter of accepting and acknowledging them.

- Everybody is bad at something! It's impossible to be good at everything.

- Everybody is good at something! It's impossible to be bad at everything.

We have to accept our strengths and our weaknesses in an objective way. You simply can't worry about your weaknesses, since we all have them. The trick is to focus on your strengths and either shrug off or overcome your weaknesses.

> *"Opportunity often comes disguised in the form of misfortune or temporary defeat."*
>
> *Mary McLeod Bethune*

KEY #8
FEAR OF FAILURE

Kakorraphiophobia is a killer! This fear is often so great that people never even attempt to dream about a goal, because the possible consequence of failure is just too darn scary. To erase this fear, you must learn to embrace it. Failure is something that you can't avoid. Failure will happen from time to time no matter what you do, so why worry about something that you can't avoid? It's like being obsessed with death; death is coming to all of us, but if you focus on it and constantly worry about it, you will never be able to focus on and enjoy living your life. Don't worry about the unavoidable; just learn to deal with it. **Failure always has a valuable lesson to teach, so don't be afraid of it. Pay attention to it!**

When you goof, don't beat yourself up. Just shrug your shoulders and ask:

1. Why didn't this work?

2. Does it work for other people?

3. How can I learn to make it work?

4. Does this goal really suit me? Do **I really** want to achieve this goal?

If the answer to #4 is **YES**, then work on answering the other three, and try again to achieve your goal. Answering these questions will give you clues on how to improvise, adapt, and overcome the issues that have kept you from success.

If the answer to question #4 is **NO**, still answer the other three questions so that you can grow. Then move on to something else. **Please read these four questions again and again until they are embedded in your mind.** If you keep these four questions in your mind, you will be able to begin to let go of your fear of failure.

You should never be afraid to fail, but you should always be afraid of not trying. Just as with life, you should never be afraid of dying but afraid of not living life to its fullest. Remember what Mel Gibson said in *Braveheart?* **"Every man dies, but not every man truly lives."** Okay, maybe that's a bit corny, but it's still true nonetheless. Humans are the only creatures on earth that live with regrets. If you wish to live your life without regrets, then you have to do your best. By doing your best, you will not leave any room for regret.

> *"God doesn't call on us to be successful;*
> *he calls on us to try."*
> ### Mother Theresa

I believe Mother Theresa has a good point here. I'm not advocating failure as an option—not at all. What I will say is that you cannot allow the "fear of failure" to be an excuse for not trying.

It's better to fall on your face after you have put your best foot forward, than

to not ever take a step and live a life of
regret.

KEY #9
OVERCOMING THE FEAR
OF FAILURE

This fear can be beaten. The one surefire way to beat the
fear of failure is to simply **do your best.** If you truly put
your best foot forward and give it your all, then you will
never have to be ashamed of failure. There is nothing wrong
with screwing up or falling short. It's inevitable! If you are
being criticized for this failure, don't get defensive. Just take
it on the chin and be confident in the fact that you did
your best. Usually, you will be able to figure out where you
went wrong and correct the situation. **If you DON'T do
your best, and you fail as a result, then you will have
something to be ashamed about.**

Another way to release yourself from the **Fear of Failure** is to
not do things for the *approval* of others. The **fear of letting
other people down** is a strong driver for the fear of failure.
If you are able to set this aside and replace it with a fear of
letting **yourself** down, then you will be able to relieve much
of the pressure. Again, the only pressure you should feel is
the pressure to do your best, not to please others with your
performance. **You can't control other people, you can only
control yourself.** If others decide to smile and offer approval,
then you may consider that to be a nice bonus. You can't make
people happy, nor can you make people like you. You can act

in such a way that people will be more likely to be attracted to who you are, but it is still their choice. You are powerless to change this fact. The best that you can do is to be your best, and it's human nature for most people to respect a person who is doing their best.

Robert Kiyosaki has a "Top 10" list for why people fail.

1. Laziness

2. Bad habits

3. Lack of education

4. Lack of experience

5. Lack of guidance

6. Lack of focus

7. Lack of determination

8. Lack of courage

9. Bad attitude

10. Bad influence from friends and family

Robert is the best selling success author on earth, so I would suggest that his list has some serious merit. The good news is that you have the ability to change any of the above points and overcome any adversity in your life. Strive to remove each of the above "top ten" points from your life one by one. With each point removed, your life will surge forward with ever-increasing speed.

> *"Success is moving from one failure to the next with enthusiasm."*
> **Sir Winston Churchill**

Anthony Robbins writes, **"There is no failure, only results."** I love this concept. With this philosophy, being afraid of failure is sort of like being afraid of the boogie man. If failure doesn't exist, then there is nothing to fear. Every successful person who I know or have read about subscribe to this philosophy on failure, and thus aren't afraid of giving a full effort toward any project. One fellow I know who is worth hundreds of millions of dollars refers to his two bankruptcies as "market research." A failed company is not a failure at all. A failed company is simply an expensive education on what works and what doesn't.

> *"Failure is the tuition that you pay for success."*
> **Walter Brunell**

If you fall flat on your face, you have not failed. What has happened is that the actions you have chosen to take have produced a negative result. When negative results occur, you simply have to step back and analyze the results so that you can adjust your actions for the next attempt, thus enabling yourself to produce a different, more positive result.

Another tool in overcoming the fear of failure is to realize that you have nothing to lose. **Whatever it is that you are trying to get—you already don't have it!** If you try to achieve something and you don't achieve it, you are no worse off. You **already** didn't achieve it. From this perspective, you have nothing to lose and everything to gain, regardless of the goal that you have set for yourself. I find great encouragement in this line of thought, and I hope that you do as well.

Charlie "Tremendous" Jones and Gregory Scott Reid wrote a great book called *Positive Impact*. In this book, they narrate a story that relates. Here is an excerpt from this wonderful book:

> **It reminds me of a friend of mine. A week or so ago, we were having lunch together at a restaurant. We spotted this beautiful woman there, and my friend said how much he'd love to go out with her. I suggested that he go over and ask her out on a date, but he said, "What if she says no?" I said, "She's already not going out with you, so you have nothing to lose here. In reality, you can only gain a date."**

 Regardless of what happens, he can't fail! He will either get a date or he won't. There is no failure; there are only results.

KEY #10
FEAR OF SUCCESS

Fear of failure is a critical challenge to overcome, but what is equally common and more difficult to understand is the **fear of success.**

The fear of success can be just as powerful as the fear of failure. Fear of success stems from people's deep belief that they don't deserve to have what they want. The main difference between fear of failure and fear of success is that:

- The **fear of failure is often a** *conscious* **fear.** People usually know that they are afraid to fail.

- **Fear of success is usually an** *unconscious* **fear.** People rarely realize that what is holding them back is the thought that they don't feel worthy of actually getting what they want.

When people who have low self-esteem unexpectedly succeed at something, they will typically react in one of two ways:

1. They will either have the sudden realization that **"success is not an accident,"** and they deserve to succeed. And thus, they go on to further accomplishments.

2. Or, they will refuse to believe that they actually deserve to have what they have just achieved, and they will often lose what they had just gained.

One of the motivators for fear of success is the **responsibility** that comes along with it. **The bigger they are, the harder they fall.** Once you achieve a higher level than you are accustomed to, you are then obligated to maintain your new status. If you don't maintain your new status, you might fear that others will think your achievement was just luck or a fluke you didn't deserve.

The higher you climb, the farther it is to fall. Scary stuff isn't it? This is why it is important to understand that **you not only deserve to achieve but that you have the ability to maintain your success.** It is also important to remember that we should attempt new and bigger things for our own benefit and not for the approval of others. **It is our responsibility for us to constantly learn and grow as individuals.**

It's healthy to realize that you have to grow to succeed. Once you have grown, you can never regress. **Wisdom can not be unlearned.**

The point is that **success is the proof of your growth**, and growth can never be taken away from you. **Growth is a lifetime asset!**

The fear of success has been the greatest challenge on my own personal path. When I first started to achieve, I had the nagging feeling that I was "faking it." When someone would give me a pat on the back, I would feel that I had them "fooled" into believing that I was a capable, successful person. I was in **success denial.** I just didn't understand or believe I deserved my accomplishments or that I was capable of even greater accomplishments.

It took a few years of doing really well both professionally and personally to gain enough perspective to see that I am successful. Once I realized I actually deserved my accomplishments, a weight was lifted. And my successes, both personal and professional, started to multiply at an increased rate. It wasn't easy to believe that the only limits on my life were set by me. It's not easy to take responsibility for our failures or our successes.

Until you are able to take responsibility for both your failure and your success, you will always be dragging an anchor behind you on your path to having the life you want.

Quotes on Failure:

- *"Fear can only prevail when victims are ignorant of the facts."*
  Thomas Jefferson

- *"Failure is simply a few errors in judgment, repeated every day."*
  Jim Rohn

- *"The worst thing one can do is not to try, to be aware of what one wants and not give in to it, to spend years in silent hurt wondering if something could have materialized—never knowing.*"

                                    Jim Rohn

KEY #11
CRITICISM IS A WONDERFUL GIFT

It takes a big person to accept criticism. Often, people are not able to distinguish between constructive and destructive criticism. Consequently, all they hear when they are criticized is an attack on their character.

Constructive criticism comes from a person who cares about you, and this person hopes to help you by shedding a light on what they perceive to be a shortcoming. This criticism is coming from a positive stance and is intended to deliver a positive message. By accepting this information, you are respecting their opinion while not necessarily agreeing with it. By realizing that you are not being attacked, you will be able to remain objective in your decision to agree or disagree with the criticism.

Destructive criticism contains a negative message and comes from a person who is trying to tear you down. If they are trying to tear you down, it isn't necessarily because they don't care about you. When one feels a need to attack, it's usually because they are insecure and feel a need to be superior to you. As with constructive criticism, there is no need to fight back. Just give their opinion the level of respect it deserves and decide to agree or disagree with the criticism. Just because they are coming from a negative stance, it doesn't mean there isn't any merit in what is being said.

We shouldn't shy away from opinions that challenge us. None of us is perfect; therefore we all should be open to criticism. **Criticism is a gift that gives you an opportunity to grow.**

KEY #12
IT'S NEVER TOO LATE

If you are worried that it's too late in your life to start making changes for the better, then let me ask you to consider this:

The sun is going to come up tomorrow morning whether you want it to or not. Time passes without any thought given toward us humans. If you wish to make the most of life, you can't let a single day pass without growth, regardless of your age. If you are still alive tomorrow morning, you will be a day older whether you like it or not. Don't waste your day—for as far as you know, it could be your last. If you have thousands of days left, then remember that time is a limited resource, and that it's meant to be used wisely. Time is incredibly precious, and non-renewable, so be cautious to not waste it.

I once heard a sixty-year-old woman saying to herself, "I wish I would have bought a coffee shop when I was still in my fifties. It's just too late to get started now." When

I heard this, I asked her what her plans were for the next twenty years. She looked at me with a slightly puzzled look and answered that she wasn't really sure. She wasn't even sure that she had twenty years left in her life. I replied to her, "Nobody can be sure that they even have tomorrow left in their life, but you also can't be sure that you won't. Time is going to pass regardless, so if you don't have any better plans over the next twenty years, you might as well go out and buy that coffee shop as soon as possible. You can always sell it later, but at least you won't end up as an eighty-year-old woman full of regrets."

Consider the story of Colonel Sanders, and his KFC™:

> Starting at the tender age of sixty-two, Colonel Sanders devoted himself to franchising his famous chicken. He drove all over the country cooking batches of chicken for restaurant owners and their employees. If the reaction was favorable, he entered into a handshake agreement on a deal that stipulated a payment to him of a nickel for each chicken meal that the restaurant sold. By 1964, Colonel Sanders had more than 600 franchised outlets that provided his chicken in the United States and Canada. That same year, he sold his interest in the company for two million dollars to a group of investors. However, he remained a public spokesman for the company and traveled all over the world on behalf of the chicken that he had made famous. By the time he died at the age of ninety, Colonel Sanders had traveled the world several times over promoting the chicken empire he had founded.

Prior to the age of sixty-two, Sanders was operating a service station in Corbin, Kentucky. Sanders began serving his secret chicken recipe to travelers who stopped at his service station. As this was a service station and not a drive through, he served his customers on his own dining table in the living quarters of the station. Most people wouldn't have taken their conviction even this far, but Sanders believed in himself and in his recipe. As a result, he died a man of great achievement instead of great regret. More importantly, **he lived fully and happily** as a result of pursuing his goals.

KEY #13
THE VICTIM MENTALITY (EGO AT ITS WORST)

Things don't happen to you, they happen around you.

If you are wounded during battle, the wound you have received was nothing personal. The person who pulled the trigger didn't shoot you because of anything you did. They shot you because it was their job to do so. The rifleman had no idea of who you are, and he had no notion of you whatsoever.

If you are a woman and you suffer through a rape, the rapist's violent actions were not a result of anything that you are or did. You didn't provoke the assault in any way; the rapist's intolerable actions were a result of his massive faults and insecurities, not yours.

When something horrible happens to us, we must take care to not let the action redefine who we are. If you are diagnosed with cancer, the worst thing you can do is to start calling yourself a cancer victim. What you are is alive, so act alive. If you have cancer in your body, and you're still breathing—then you are already a cancer survivor. You don't have to wait for remission to be a survivor; you are a survivor from the moment you get the diagnosis. Choosing to be a survivor instead of a victim will put you in the correct mental state required to travel forward toward perfect health. The choice of a positive state over a negative state is always available to you regardless of the circumstance.

There are countless stories of detainees from Nazi death camps who where in good spirits and who never gave up the hope of survival. The people who were fortunate enough not to be murdered and who maintained the choice of staying in a positive state were the ones who managed to survive starvation and death. If a death camp survivor can refuse to be a victim, then you certainly can as well.

If you are feeling sorry for yourself, then try to imagine someone who has dealt with far worse circumstances yet never complains. These people understand that they have the power to choose their state of mind.

Eckhart Tolle's book, *A New Earth,* teaches us that it is our attachment to our ego or our false sense of self that fuels the victim mentality. Being a victim is like being a part of an exclusive club that awards us with the attention of others. When you are a victim, you rush to any willing ear that will let you tell your story. What you are seeking is sympathy so that your self-made label of being a victim will be reinforced.

The victim mentality is a very strong negative mental state. Being in this state causes you to constantly lay blame or point fingers at others. Victims don't want to see that they can choose to not be a victim. Unconsciously, they want the sympathy, the attention of others, and the affirmation from others that they are victims—and therefore special.

Being aware of the victim mentality will cause it to melt away inside you. Being a victim is a notion that comes from the ego, and when you are aware of your ego, the ego then disappears in proportion to your level of awareness.

In all choices of positive over negative, you are choosing to be aware of your ego. The ego is always manifested by negative energy, and therefore it always has a negative effect on your life. **The more aware that you are of the difference between positive and negative speech, actions, and mind-sets, the more able you will be to choose the positive option.** Every time you make the choice to be positive, you are making a decision that is free of your ego. Choosing positive over negative is choosing happiness over misery in your life. When you are living a happy life, any lives you touch are lifted by your mere presence. When you are living in misery, you are bringing down anyone who comes in contact with you.

The victim is always miserable, and the world is always against him. The

victim sees enemies where there are only friends and treachery where there is only compassion.

The victim believes that the whole world revolves around him. If he gets a flat tire, the tire company sold him a faulty tire, and they knew better. They just wanted to get rid of their defective stock, so when they saw him coming, they took advantage of him. They knew full well that it was no darn good! The victim is now going to be late for a meeting because of those crooks at the tire shop.

If a non-victim gets a flat tire, he just sorts out the problem and moves on without a second thought. The non-victim is likely to not even bring up the flat-tire story to his wife as it was a complete non-issue. The victim, however, will add the flat tire to the long list of other situations where he believes he was cheated. The cumulative list of resentment is incredibly toxic and unhealthy to the victim. Even the physical health of the victim will be affected by the massive negative energy. Being in a constantly negative state diminishes the immune system, leaving victims susceptible to illness. The unavoidable illnesses are then interpreted by the victim as proof that they are special and are singled out by the world to be a doormat.

When you meet a victim, simply try to be aware that they are enslaved by their egos and they just don't know any better. They can't see the negative effects that are caused by their mind-set. The victim can't take responsibility for negative results, but can only lay blame on others. **Negativity is blinding in all of its forms and manifestations.**

CHAPTER 2
UNDERSTANDING YOUR PURPOSE

KEY #14
DHARMA

In the Hindu religion, there is a sharp focus on **Dharma**. Choosing your Dharma is choosing to walk the path set for you by the Supreme Being. If you follow your Dharma, you will no longer be a fish out of water, or a round peg trying to fit in a square hole. When you are doing what you are meant to do, you will then be utilizing your natural skill sets and talents; thus, success will be inevitable. Finding your Dharma is like falling in love. If you're ready for it to happen, then when it happens, you will just know. And nobody will be able to talk you out of it. If you aren't sure of what it is you should be doing, just make sure that you are in the ball park. Close is good enough for a start.

One way to find your Dharma is to write a list of what you **don't** want in your life. Most people have an easier time identifying what they don't want than what they do want. It will still take courage to cut these items out of your life, but at least you will have a list to use as a reference when you are deciding on one path over another. The closer you are to your Dharma, the easier and more enjoyable your life path will be.

The best example I can think of to illustrate Dharma is to talk about my dog, Abby. Abby is an English Springer Spaniel or "Springer" for short. Springers are born and bred to hunt and flush out game birds such as grouse and pheasants, which is the prime purpose for me choosing this breed. From her normal behavior, most people would assume that Abby is a happy dog when they meet her. She is a bundle of excitement when she greets every guest, and she is even more excited if she recognizes who you are. She's an indoor dog who is well cared for, pampered, and loved as much as any dog could hope for. It's true that our little Abby is generally a happy dog who is in good spirits. However, she wasn't born and bred to be a family lap dog.

Abby suffers from arthritis, and at home she needs help to get up on to the couch or into her favorite chair. She climbs the stairs with some difficulty and discomfort, but she can do it on her own. In this environment where she is merely content, this is the demeanor of our precious friend. One would never suspect what she is capable of when she is placed in the environment she was born and bred to be in.

When the short two weeks of pheasant season comes around, I'm ready for it. The pheasant area is a two-hour drive south of my home. Consequently, for me to be there for first legal shooting light, I have to get up bright and early. The moment I grab my hunting jacket and my shotgun, Abby perks up and starts to look like a different dog. Suddenly she is able to fly up and down the stairs without any sign of pain, and she has a look of anticipation in her eyes that can only be described as sheer joy. On the drive down to the pheasant area, she calms down. But as soon as we get within ten minutes of our regular area, Abby starts to fuss with anticipation. Even though we only go about three times a season, she recognizes every tree and bush within a fifteen mile radius. By the time we start down the final dirt road, Abby is jumping out of her skin with excitement. The moment I park, I open the door for her, and she bolts out of the vehicle as if she were on fire.

Once I get all of my gear prepared and the clock tells me that it's time for legal shooting light, we're off to hunt. My little arthritic dog runs full out, weaving in and out of the bushes without any encouragement for three hours straight. Even in the deepest bush (which Springers are renowned for), Abby will crash through the thistles and leap over the logs and deadfall as if she were four years younger and much fitter than she actually is. When Abby does find a bird or rabbit, she lets out an uncontainable yelp of excitement as she chases after it for me. Each time she finds a bird, she is re-energized and unstoppable.

This is the power of Dharma. Hunting is what Abby was born and bred to do. It is the reason she was placed on this earth. Although she can be relatively happy without hunting, she will never be so happy as when she is hunting.

When you are traveling the path you were meant to travel, the one you were designed for, you will then be at your happiest as well. If I could hunt with Abby all year round, I would. It brings me enormous joy to watch the excitement she experiences during the hunt. Even when we aren't successful at finding any game, she is still far happier pursuing her purpose than being at home on the couch. **She doesn't lament that she has failed in her attempt; instead, she relishes the fact that she had the opportunity to try.**

> *"One's real life is often the life that one does not lead."*
>
> Oscar Wilde

> *"A musician must make music, an artist must paint, and a poet must write if he is to be ultimately at peace with himself."*
>
> Abraham Maslow

KEY #15
THE RESPONSIBILITY OF TALENT

One of the reasons I am driven to succeed at my endeavors is that I feel a responsibility to do so.

> *"Gods gift to us is our talents; our gift to God is using them."*
>
> Unknown

I always knew I had talents, and once I was able to identify them and their potential value, I was able to find my path, my Dharma. If I were to ignore my path and my potential, I feel that I would be slapping God in the face.

Ignoring your talents is like blowing a million dollar payout from your parents' life insurance policy on a weekend in Vegas. This would be a massive disrespect to the memory of your parents and their many years of careful diligence paying into an insurance policy to ensure a better future for you.

Talents are a precious gift that all people have received to varying degrees. Sadly, most people take their gift for granted and never choose to implement and thus enjoy their talents.

What are your talents? Everyone has them, yet not everyone is fully aware of them. **We can all elevate ourselves, and the most rewarding way to do so is by discovering and utilizing our talents.**

> *"I know of no more encouraging fact*
> *than the unquestioned ability of a man*
> *to elevate his life by conscious endeavor."*
> *Thoreau*

For the first time in human history, we live in a global society that provides abundant opportunity for almost everybody. There are difficulties for all, but not so much as to drown out anyone's ability to pursue the opportunities before them. **What a shame it is to have talents that are never realized, yet most of society commits this grave sin under a blanket of excuses.**

> *"The real source of wealth and capital in this new era is not material things; it is in the human mind, the human spirit, the human imagination, and our own faith in the future. That's the magic of a free society—everyone can move forward and prosper because wealth comes from within."*
>
> **Steve Forbes**

All of us have an urge, sometimes a secret urge to find our Dharma. Many refuse to even look for their Dharma or admit that they have one. Are you one those people who complains about your job or your business? If so, this is probably because you are not in a situation that uses and pushes your talents and potential. Not all of us can become billionaires, but most can become millionaires. I'm using money here as a measuring stick, but this concept applies to your wealth of happiness and contentment. It's fear that keeps us from admitting our potential and our talents. It is this same fear that presents itself to appear as **laziness.**

> *"There is no such thing as lazy people, there is only the uninspired."*
>
> **unknown**

Many couch potatoes are on the couch because they have simply given up. They don't know where to start and feel there is no point in trying because they won't win regardless of what they do. The attitude is: "What's the point in setting myself up for disappointment?"

*"Men are made stronger on the realization
that the helping hand that they need is at
the end of their own right arm."*
Sidney J. Philips

Other people will simply succumb to their fear of failure
and come up with any and every excuse in the book as
to why they "can't" do it. These people will rationalize
with themselves and others to explain that the size of the
stones in their path are simply too large to climb, never
admitting they were the ones who threw the stones there
in the first place. It's amazing how people will protect their
self-limiting beliefs. If you challenge their beliefs or try to
offer solutions to their so-called "problems," their tendency
will be to resist with a mighty force.

If you try to offer examples of those who have already done
what these folks wish that they could do, you will likely be
resisted by excuses, imaginary obstacles, and rationalization.
The skeptics will tell you that the people who "did it" were
just in the right time and the right place. It's common for
skeptics to attempt to trivialize success by saying, *"They
were just lucky."*

Being aware of the fact that these are normal and predictable
responses to *"the truth"* will arm you against the influence
of misinformation and self-limiting beliefs. **Self-limiting
beliefs can be incredibly persuasive and potentially
very dangerous to your success.** They are like a super-
contagious disease, and you must take precautions to avoid
being infected by them. When choosing an environment

to spend time in, ensure that it is not contaminated by self-doubting, self-limiting influences. Just as you wouldn't go swimming in shark-infested waters, take heed to ensure the crowd you run with is a positive one.

Although potentially dangerous, I have found that negative people can also be great teachers. You can learn what is correct by hearing and seeing the negative results produced by negative people. Understanding how it is that they achieved those negative results will allow you to see how the results could have easily been positive had the energy used towards the goal been positive. These people are proof that **positive or negative energy produces positive or negative results**. Another layer of armor you can wear is to realize that when people try to keep your feet on the ground, it's usually because they don't want you to surpass them. Not many people are mature enough to offer encouragement to someone who is about to surpass them.

KEY #16
TALENTS ARE OPPORTUNITIES, NOT ENTITLEMENTS

If you have not already seen the movie *Evan Almighty*, then I suggest that you do. It's a great comedy, and there are good lessons to be learned from this film. Morgan Freeman's God character had this to share:

> "If you pray for patience, God doesn't give you patience; he gives you the **opportunity** to be patient.

If you pray for courage, God won't give you courage; he
will give you the **opportunity** to be courageous."

Your talents are opportunities, not entitlements. If you
have ever watched *American Idol*, or any of the other
Idol competitions, you surely would remember at least
one contestant who felt that he/she was entitled to win.
These people would strut around with an arrogant air, just
waiting to be rewarded for their talent. What they didn't
understand is that talent alone is just not enough. You need
to have many more tools in the tool pouch.

If you are waiting around for someone to swoop into your
life to give you that "big break" by recognizing your talents,
then you are likely going to be waiting for a long time. If
you feel that talent alone entitles you to a life of showcasing
your talents, then again, you will be disappointed. It's true
that some people, like the beautiful Pamela Anderson, are
just "discovered," but for every Pam Anderson, there are a
thousand others who had to claw and scrape their way to
the top. Even in Pam's case, being discovered was only the
opportunity. Pamela had to do the work to make the most
of the opportunity and to be successful. Many people would
have blown the chance that Pam was given, or they would
not have had the courage to jump on the opportunity.

Your talent is a doorway to a goal, not a winning lottery
ticket that guarantees your goal. You can be disempowered
by letting others decide whether or not to value your talents,
or you can be empowered by taking your future into your
own hands.

Somewhere out there, the next Mozart, Jimmy Hendrix, Einstein, or Stephen Hawking is riding the bus to the widget factory while scores of others with far less talent are living the life of a superstar. Many people have succeeded at ventures where others with far more talent have failed. Talent is just not enough. **You must take action to implement your talents, or they will just waste away in the cellar of your soul.**

> *"The best way to predict the future is to create it."*
>
> *unknown*

What are your talents? If you know what they are, then— what are you waiting for? If you are waiting for courage, you will find it by continuing to educate yourself through books or courses. The more you grow, the more confident you will feel. Instead of waiting for courage, you can just go on faith that things will work out, and jump NOW. The courage and confidence will come later. Just act, take a deep breath, and jump!

KEY #17
SKILL SETS

Success, overcoming fear, and effectively achieving goals are all learnable skill sets. All of the keys that are shared in this book are learnable.

If I was plopped into the middle of a *McDonald's* kitchen and told to start cooking burgers and fries, I'd be totally lost. I wouldn't have a clue what to do, but only because I haven't put in the time to develop the required skill set. I'm sure that there are not many people out there who don't have the confidence to be a competent back line cook at *McDonald's*, yet few have the confidence to acquire the skill sets required for great personal success. This is what I know to be true: **Both skill sets are equally attainable.**

The self-limiting belief of "I'm not qualified" will dictate the type of pursuit you will have the confidence to chase. **You have to understand that your resume can only show what you have done; it cannot show your potential.** The resume is only a reflection of the past, and although the past is a good predictor of the future, you have the ability to grow at any moment you choose. No resume can illustrate your growth potential.

What if your resume only shows all of the wrong paths you have ever walked? How is this going to demonstrate the fact that a different path which compliments your skill sets would allow you to soar above the crowd? Resumes simply cannot show your true potential. It is improbable you will ever achieve more than you believe you are capable of achieving. You can lie to yourself and call yourself a "realist," but, really, you're just a pessimist. The chances are that you are dragging down others around you with your negative view of your own life.

The skills you don't yet have today can be acquired for tomorrow. Acquiring a new skill is nothing more than a small challenge to overcome. Any puzzle that is placed in front of you can be solved.

A very dear friend of mine once bought a beat up, worn out Jeep CJ5. The thing didn't even have tires on it, was full of rust, and was missing many parts. Michael was able to get this junker for $350.00 with the intention of parking it in his garage and rebuilding it from the ground up.

Now it must be understood here that Mike was neither a mechanic nor an auto body technician. In fact, Mike had absolutely no idea at all of how to rebuild an engine or refinish a vehicle's surface. The only thing Mike knew for certain was that whatever the challenge, he could figure out a solution.

The easy part was to disassemble and label every nut, bolt, wire, and screw from the vehicle. The old Jeep was stripped to the frame, the body was removed, and the engine was pulled.

With the Jeep fully pulled apart, the next step was for Mike to decide on the order in which he would solve each of the challenges he had just created for himself. Using logic and common sense, Mike learned one skill at a time, and he bought all of the required tools to do the job. The only applicable skill that pre-existed for this project was Mike's scant experience as a welder almost twenty years prior.

The end result was that of a fully rebuilt machine. There were mistakes that had to be re-done, and it wasn't the fanciest paint job. But overall, that Jeep looked fantastic.

What does your Jeep look like? Perhaps your Jeep is the piano that's sitting in the corner of your living room. Maybe you're the person who's been thinking about learning to play for years, but just never got around to it. Maybe your Jeep is a surf board or perhaps a parachute. What is the goal you have been procrastinating about because it would require skills which you don't yet have? **If you keep making excuses, the only possible result is future regrets.**

KEY #18
ATTITUDE

*It's a fine line between attitude and perspective. Have you ever heard the expression, **"Your attitude, not your aptitude will determine your altitude"**? Zig Ziglar*

Using the "maze/balloon" metaphor, you can see how your altitude increases your perspective. So from this angle, the two are interwoven.

Have you ever been told that you had a "bad attitude"? I find it odd when I hear people say this as it doesn't explain what a **"bad attitude"** actually is. Basically, **a negative attitude will sink you, and a positive attitude will allow you to fly.** So if you hear someone saying that you have a bad attitude, chances are that you are being perceived as negative.

Perspective is the position you are in when you look at a situation (point of view).

Attitude is the **CHOICE** of positive or negative energy that you use when you assess a situation. Here is an example:

Jack and Jill went up a hill to fetch a pail of water. Jack saw that the well was dry, and **chose** to throw an angry fit. He was yelling at the well, yelling at his bucket, and finally he shouted down the hill at the fool that sent them up this darn hill in the first place. (Though the "fool" couldn't hear Jack from way down in the town). After all the hollering, Jack plopped his grumpy butt on the ground and proceeded to mutter his frustration, with only his bucket to listen.

Jill tried to calm him and reassure him that this was a minor deal, but Jack just got angry at Jill for not joining him in his rant. Jill decided it was no use trying to talk to Jack, so she just left him on the hill to fester in his frustration. Jill knew she couldn't go home with an empty bucket, so she marched down the hill and up another hill that had another well. It too was dry so she just shrugged her shoulders and said aloud, "There's not much that I can do about a dry well, and throwing a fit like Jack did won't improve the situation, so I'll just have to keep looking, and check the next well."

With a click of her heels, she decided to happily enjoy the unexpected challenge of filling her bucket with water. She skipped down the hill to try again. On Jill's third ascent of her third hill to check her third well, she found success. Jill couldn't help but to feel pride in the fact that she didn't give up, and that her

perseverance rewarded her with a bucket of water that she could carry home with pride. Jill also felt just a little sad for Jack because she wished that he hadn't given up so easily. He too could have known the feeling of pride that she was now enjoying.

When she got home, she told her parents of the effort required, and her parents were proud of her tenacity and positive attitude. Poor Jack didn't have a very warm reception when he returned home with his empty pail. Jack let himself down, and he let down his entire family, who was counting on the water to drink with their dinner. Jack's "bad attitude" meant that the family would go thirsty that day.

Let us boil this down:

- A positive attitude fuels perseverance.

- Perseverance fuels success.

- Success gives you pride in yourself and a positive social status.

- A negative attitude is fuel for giving up.

- Giving up fuels failure.

- Failure **that is due to giving up** makes you ashamed of yourself and results in regret. (Don't mix this up with failure after doing your best! There is no shame in failing if you did your best).

A positive attitude is a key element in achieving any goal. Without it, you're swimming upstream. When people tend to adopt a negative attitude, they also tend to blame others for their problems. If you blame others for your problems, then you are playing the "victim" role. **As long as you choose to be a victim, you can never choose to be a winner.**

It's important for me to be clear here. Saying that you "choose to be a victim" doesn't mean that you choose to be victimized. When something horrible happens to you, I'm not saying that it's your fault or that you have brought it on yourself. What I am saying is that you have a choice of how to deal with the fact that something nasty has just happened.

A positive attitude allows you to be a problem solver because, instead of focusing on everything that's wrong, it allows you to focus on everything that is right, and on the possibilities. A negative attitude will always blind you to the possibilities that are right under your nose.

Quotes on Attitude

- *"Positive thinking will let you do everything better than negative thinking will."*

  Zig Ziglar

- *"Let others lead small lives, but not you. Let others argue over small things, but not you. Let others cry over small hurts, but not you. Let others leave their future in someone else's hands, but not you."*

  Jim Rohn

- *"Attitude is more than just being positive. It's a way of looking at life, ours and everybody's. It is said to be Everything because it is Everything. It defines who we are and what we become!"*

  Alvin Law

- *"You miss 100 percent of the shots that you don't take."*

  Wayne Gretzky

KEY #19
WHAT DO YOU REALLY TRULY WANT?

The answer to this simple question will provide you with a focus. It's an extremely scary thing to answer, because once you admit your dreams to yourself, you then have to decide: *Do I have the guts to move toward my goal or not?*

To answer the question "What do I really want?" first remove the pressure. I suggest imagining that you have found Aladdin's lamp, and the genie has offered you three life goals. All that you have to do is to choose the three in order of preference. Ask yourself, **"What would I do if I knew that I couldn't fail?"** You should also ask, **"What would I do if I didn't need the money?"** Answering these questions doesn't have to be scary. Once you have the tools for overcoming the fears of both success and failure, you will then have the courage to try in the face of failure. Courage is just as rewarding as Aladdin's lamp. With courage, all you need to do is identify your needs, wants, and desires, then **go for it!** Forget all of the "what ifs" of failure. **What others have done before you, so can you.**

Some people are blessed with a certainty of direction. These people know what they want to do with their lives, and they just go for it without distraction. Most of us, however, are less sure of the direction we wish to take, and therefore we bounce around from path to path hoping to stumble across the right path for us (Dharma). I was thirty-three years old before I found a direction that was right for me, though it was clear to some of my closest friends many years prior which path I should explore. Once I finally found my path, I flew down it with blatant enthusiasm and never looked back.

> *"Find the environment where you thrive. We would probably never have heard of Tiger Woods if there were no golf courses."*
>
> *Robert Kiyosaki*

You may not know what you want yet, but **the lessons in this book will help you find the courage to admit your**

goals to yourself and the wisdom to allow your dreams to manifest. When you find your passion, there is little that can stop you from following it. Here is an example:

Troy, a very good friend of mine, knew that he wanted to be a pilot since he was a kid. Once he was out of high school, there wasn't any struggle or confusion in deciding his next step. He simply applied for his student loan, applied for flight school, and off he went! **His goal was clear, so the steps he had to take to achieve his goal were equally clear.**

After two years of very difficult courses, Troy graduated flight school and landed himself a job flying sky divers so that he could build his flight hours. The job barely paid anything, but he needed to build his hours or he wouldn't have a flight career. Eight hundred low-paid hours later, Troy started climbing the flight ladder by getting better and better flying jobs with the ultimate goal of being an airline pilot. Not once do I remember Troy complaining about the low pay or the long hours. He was grateful for the opportunity to fly, and he kept his eyes on the prize.

> *"Obstacles are the troubling things*
> *that you see when you lose sight of your*
> *goals."*
>
> *Henry Ford*

Being a commercial airline pilot is one of the most competitive jobs on earth. Most people who want the job never have the guts to even try for it. To fly one of the "big birds" is like making it onto a professional sports team. It means that you are the cream of the crop—the top dog in your field. By having a clear goal, and through sheer determination, Troy finally made it to the big show. Today he is an Air Canada captain.

The purpose of this true story is to illustrate how important it is to know what you want. **If Troy hadn't been totally certain of his goal, he never would have achieved it.** It's impossible to commit years of your life to achieving a difficult goal unless there is not a "Plan B." Once you know what you want, you have to **find the courage to imagine how it would feel once you actually have it.**

KEY #20

WHY DO YOU WANT WHAT YOU WANT?

The short answer is "for pleasure and happiness." All endeavors are to achieve gratification of some kind. Whether it is power, pleasure, money, or status, every endeavor is inspired by the want of gratification. Even charity can be self-serving since you receive the status and gratification associated with giving.

To understand **why** you want is to understand **if** you should want the things that you are trying to acquire. Not all pursuits of pleasure are going to benefit you. An extreme example of this is drug use. A crack addict will do or say just about anything to get his next chemical pleasure fix. The continued pursuit of this pleasure will inevitably result in the lethal demise of the crack addict. On the outside looking in, it's easy to see that the addict should stop. But of course the addict doesn't have our same perspective, so he is not always able to see that he should stop or see how to stop.

If you are pursuing something that won't improve your life either directly or indirectly, then maybe you should consider a different pursuit. Is the pleasure you are seeking going to elevate your life or just fill your garage with meaningless toys? Not that it is a crime to indulge in a few toys, but the chances are the toys won't give you the pleasure you are seeking.

Often, the pursuit of expensive toys is motivated by the want of status or the temporary gratification associated with a major purchase. If the toys are purchased as a mechanism for creating positive memories with your family and friends, then you have made a good purchase. If the motivation is other than the intention of using the toy to create positive memories with your family and friends, then you have not made a good purchase. Even if you can afford to buy the toys with cash and you won't be financially burdened by the purchase, the object is still an empty thing on which you have just wasted your money.

Let me explain this a little more. If a pursuit is intended to result in pleasure and happiness, then any result other than pleasure and happiness is a failure of that pursuit. Here's an example: if you have purchased a new motorcycle, and the only function of this motorcycle is to look nice in your garage, then it has failed to provide you with a sense of satisfaction, pleasure, and happiness. This motorcycle is then clearly a poor purchase as it has not provided the payback that was intended. If you ride this motorcycle with friends and family—or even on your own, and thus derive satisfaction and enjoyment as a result—then this is a good purchase.

Sticking with the motorcycle example, if you constantly buy toy after toy and are always envious of those who have what you don't, then you will never be satisfied by any amount of toys. In this case, the urge to purchase is a problem that needs to be understood and addressed. Once the underlying urge is understood, there will no longer be an insatiable urge to purchase toys.

An attitude of gratitude should always be observed in regards to the material things we have. If you feel gratitude for what you have, then you will feel satisfied. If you do not feel gratitude, then you will always want more and you will never be satisfied.

Do you have pursuits that are for the benefit of others and not just yourself? **The highest and most fulfilling pursuits are those for the benefit of others.**

Enjoyment and amusement are often sought to provide a substitute for happiness. True happiness comes from within, from loving yourself and your life. Chasing amusement through material items, liquor, pornography, movies, or TV is just a substitute for happiness. Thus, the saying: "Money can't buy happiness." **Money can only buy the substitutes for happiness and the distractions from pain.**

If we were to put 1/100th of the effort into being truly happy that we put into amusement, then there would not be nearly as many anti-depressants being prescribed. True happiness comes from being the best human you can be—not from being the human with the most toys. Being the best human you can be means learning how to not be angry with others or yourself. It means never gossiping, always doing your best in every situation, and always being a better person today than you were yesterday.

Most of all, being happy means accepting and loving yourself for who you are. Nothing you can put on your credit card will make you feel that way.

Having the items you want only adds to your life if you are grateful for them. This is why it is important to understand the **"why"** of what we want. My wish for this book is to do more than just fill up your garage with cool toys. I wish to provide you with the understanding of how to enjoy those toys.

When you are choosing what you want, remember the reasons why you want. If the **"what"** doesn't reflect the intended **"why,"** then you should reconsider your goals. What is the point of achieving anything if it doesn't add happiness to your life?

CHAPTER 3
THE TOOLS TO REALIZE YOUR PURPOSE

KEY #21
THE LAW OF ATTRACTION

"All things whatsoever ye pray and ask
for, believe that ye have received them,
and ye shall receive them."
Mark 11:24

This key can be an incredibly tough pill to swallow, but it's completely true all the same. The law of attraction has been written about as far back as written records can be found. This law, like the law of gravity, works whether you understand it or not. Several books and dozens of chapters of other books have been written about this universal law. Oprah Winfrey promoted the movie and book, *The Secret*, which is dedicated to sharing this amazing concept. I suggest that you go online to find the streaming video of *The Secret*, or get the DVD. It does a far better job of explaining the **law of attraction** than I ever could in a short chapter. I use this law to my advantage daily, and it has made a huge contribution to my life.

Boiled down, the law of attraction states, **"If you can imagine what it would <u>feel like</u> to have what you want,**

then you will attract this thing into your life." You have to experience the feeling of actually having what you want for it to work, but work it does.

From a psychological stand point, "feeling as though you already have it" is a trigger for your mind. When you pull this trigger, you put your mind into a resourceful and winning mind-set. If you already feel as though you have what you want, then it's natural to start acting as though you have it. If you start acting as though you have what you want, then you will tap into your resourcefulness, and the actions which you choose to take will get you what you want.

KEY #22
BE-DO-HAVE

As the world renowned achievement coach Richard Robbins once taught me, Be-Do-Have is the direction of the flow of life. Once you understand the Law of Attraction, Be-Do-Have starts to make a lot of sense. Here is how this works:

- You have to first **BE** the person that you wish to be.

- You then will naturally act and **DO** as you are. Your actions will reflect the person that you are **being** because who "you are" determines the actions that you will take.

- As a result of your actions, you will naturally **HAVE** the things that you want in your life.

Most people try to go against the flow and swim upstream their whole lives. Have you ever noticed that the people who seem to have it all seem to have it easily? This is because they are going with the flow and allowing success to occur. You don't have to chase success; you just have to allow it to happen. **Who you decide to be will determine what is attracted into your life.**

> *"Be as you wish to seem."*
>
> **Socrates**

KEY# 23
THINK-FEEL-DO

The way you think determines how you feel, and the way you feel determines how you act. We are emotional creatures, and we make most decisions based on our feelings. If your thoughts are focused on negative things, you will then feel negative, and your actions will be negative. If you are focused on positive things, you will feel positive, and your actions will be positive. This is why attitude is so powerful and why it's so important to be conscious of your thoughts.

- If you are thinking about what you "**don't** want," then that's what will be attracted into your life.

- If you are thinking about "what you **do** want," then that's what will be attracted into your life.

This is an incredibly well-researched topic, and there is a mountain of literature dedicated to this concept. The sooner you allow yourself to accept this truth, the sooner you will find peace in your life. Be conscious of your thoughts, and your life will instantly change for the better. **The law of attraction is a magic pill that works instantly!** All you have to do is choose to take advantage of this law, and the results will appear immediately.

> *"The happiness of your life depends on the quality of your thoughts. Therefore, guard accordingly and take care that you entertain no notions unsuitable to virtue and reasonable nature."*
>
> *Marcus Antonius*

Negative thoughts blind us from opportunity. **Negativity is like having a burlap sack over our heads every time an opportunity walks by**. Simply remove the sack from your head, and you will see the opportunities that have always been right in front of you. This is true for everyone. Here is an example of some positive and negative states of being.

Negative (–) Destructive   **Positive (+) Constructive**

Negative (–) Destructive	Positive (+) Constructive
Pursue	Attract
Taking	Giving
Superior	Equal
Have to	Choose to
Persuade	Educate
Pessimistic	Optimistic
Calculating	Candid

Cheap	Generous
Suspicious	Observant
Conceit	Humble
Critical	Curious
Resentful	Forgiving
Entitled	Thankful
Envious	Grateful

If you find that your thoughts are often in the negative column, then try to replace those thoughts with their opposites in the positive column. It really is that simple.

How you think determines how you feel, and how you feel determines how you act.

KEY #24
VOCABULARY

One sure way to adjust your attitude is to adjust your vocabulary. You must discipline yourself to eliminate unhealthy words from your vocabulary. Negative words carry negative energy. These words not only harm you, but they harm everyone around you. For the sake of yourself, your family, and your friends, it is imperative that you are cognizant of your influence on others, both positive and negative. How you use your words and the words you choose matter! Whoever came up with the "sticks and stones" thing was well intentioned, but dead wrong.

Here are some examples of unhealthy words, and their alternatives.

Negative (−) Destructive	Positive (+) Constructive
Can't	Can
Lucky	Ability
Difficult	Challenging
Scarcity	Abundance
Stupid	Smart
Failure	Negative Results
Failure	Delayed Success
Victim	Survivor
Excuses	Responsibility
Try	Will

Just as you have to be conscious of your thoughts, you must be equally conscious of your words. Thoughts and words contain energy, both destructive and constructive. **Choosing your thoughts and words carefully is choosing to construct or destruct your life.** This is also why it's best to avoid excessive swearing.

One of my absolute favorite books is *The Four Agreements: A Practical Guide to Personal Freedom* by Don Miguel Ruiz. In this amazing book, Ruiz states that the first agreement is to "**be impeccable with your word.**" This first agreement alone is enough to transform anyone's life. If your words are always positive and never meant to harm others, then you will be impeccable with your word. Ruiz emphasizes the power of the word and that it is our responsibility to be aware of the power of our words. If you wish to have positive things in your life, then you must be a positive person. Like attracts like. If you are constantly negative, then you will constantly attract negativity into your life.

> *"Speak clearly, if you speak at all; carve*
> *every word before you let it fall."*
> **Oliver Wendell Holmes**

KEY #25
ACT "AS IF"

To get what you want, you sometimes have to act "as if" you already have it.

To expand further on the Law of Attraction, we must further explore the power of our actions.

As previously shared:

> *"Feeling as though you already have it" is a trigger for your mind. When you pull this trigger, your mind puts you into a winning mind-set. If you already feel as though you have what you want, then it's natural to start acting as though you have it. If you start acting as though you have what you want, then the actions you choose to take will get you what you want.*

The Law of Attraction is also explained by this concept.

- Feel "as if"
- Think "as if"
- Act "as if"

Acting "as if" can only be done if you have first started feeling "as if" and thinking "as if."

Self-doubt happens to all of us from time to time. When you doubt yourself, you have to tell yourself and everyone around you that you are well on your way to achieving your goals. This isn't being delusional; this is having the correct mind-set to achieve your goals. It's all about perspective and mind-set.

In the movie *The Boiler Room*, Ben Affleck's character gives a powerful speech to the new recruits. In this speech, he tells them to **"act as if."** Although they were not yet accomplished stock brokers, they never would join the high achievers until they were able to **"act as if"** they were already a part of the club. This isn't "faking it"; it's a tool to put you in the correct mind-set. This is the same technique used by coaches of professional sports teams during locker room talks before a big game. The coach will pump up the team by telling them that they **"already are champions"** (regardless of the fact that they have yet to win a championship). The coach may say something such as:

The trophy is yours; it's within your grasp. All you have to do is go out there and take it! The other team sure isn't going to give it to you without a fight, so go and take what is rightfully yours, this is your time!

The coach isn't tricking his team or manipulating them; he's putting them into a **winning mindset**. We humans are emotional creatures. Sometimes we need a little affirmation that we are good enough and able to achieve what we want. If a team goes into a championship game not believing they are "champions," then they won't have much hope of actually winning.

Let us sum up what we have just learned.

- Perspective and mindset will float you or sink you.

- A healthy, positive mindset is essential to accomplish any goal.

- With a little wisdom, we can have the strength to ignore those who would see us fail.

- If you refuse to be a VICTIM, you choose to be a CHAMPION!

KEY #26
BURN YOUR BRIDGES AND COMMIT

Once you have committed yourself to getting what you want, jump in with both feet and go for it. If you only go halfway, if you just dip your toes in the lake to test the water, then you'll never achieve anything worthwhile. If you want something, you have to commit totally. It's like sky diving, you can't just stick your foot out of the plane and test the air. If you want to skydive, then you have to jump.

I remember my first jump and the vision of the plane flying away from me—now, that is what I call a commitment! There is no turning back, no "Plan B," just me plummeting through the air achieving my goal with no possible way to fail. Once I jumped, failure was not an option.

The more difficult a goal, the more you have to totally commit. You can't take half measures; you can't live within your comfort zone and just dabble at your goal while you keep another full-time job to pay the bills in the meantime. **If you are trying to multi-task too much and do a little of everything, then you will end up doing a lot of nothing**. We all have to multi-task to a point. However, when you have a challenging goal in front of you, it will demand the majority of your attention and focus to achieve that goal.

KEY #27
FOCUS

"A person who aims at nothing is sure to hit it."

Unknown

Once you have committed yourself to achieving a goal, you cannot allow yourself to get distracted by new, interesting opportunities. **If you don't want to be a flake and a quitter, then you have to finish what you start before you go onto the next round of your life.** A good example of this is a former colleague who was one course short of his university bachelor's degree. He committed almost four years of his life to a goal that he didn't achieve. Some people will say that a degree is just a piece of paper, but what a degree proves is that you can finish what you start.

A degree doesn't tell the world about how smart you are, it tells the world about your character and your strength of commitment. It isn't easy to stay focused on a single goal for four long years. Any degree has value, regardless of whether or not you end up working in a related field. The feeling of accomplishment derived from any goal that you achieve can never be taken away from you.

There is power in the ability to focus your energy. As Alexander Graham Bell once said about the subject:

"Concentrate all of your thoughts upon the work at hand. The suns rays do not burn until brought into a sharp focus."

A singular mind is what has been responsible for all of the world's great achievements throughout history. Think of focus as having a one-track mind. If there is only one track for the train to go on, then there is only one destination that the train can possibly reach. Each time you are distracted by an unexpected crossroad that comes up, you will be steering away from your original goal. If you make the decision to **never take your eyes off the prize**, then you will stay on track and reach your destination far more quickly.

If you are on the right track (your Dharma), then you won't have much trouble staying focused on the task at hand. The more you travel along a track that doesn't suit you, the less you will be able to stay focused on the task at hand.

KEY #28
SACRIFICE

You can't always have your cake and eat it, too. To get what you want, you will likely be faced with the decision to let go of something else.

When you are faced with this choice, simply ask, **"What do I want more?"** When you have to let go of one thing to achieve another, do it with determination and certainty. Once you let go, don't dwell on the "what ifs." "What if I woulda?" is a question that will distract you from your goal. **All that matters is what is to come, where you are going, and how to get there.** Instead of looking at what you are letting go of as something that you are going to miss, look at it as something that is holding you back. This way you will be happy to let it go, and it won't feel like a sacrifice at all. If you don't do this, then you will miss what you've lost. If you miss what you've lost, then you may well abandon your goal in order to regain what it is that you have given up.

Arnold Schwarzenegger was a world champion bodybuilder because of the following four key things:

- Determination

- Commitment

- Sacrifice

- Focus

Arnold didn't worry about all of the things he was missing out on, such as partying with his friends, chocolate ice cream, or his social life. He knew that if he was to be the best, everything else would have to wait until he achieved his goal. Anyone or anything that stood in his way became an enemy that he would simply defeat so that he could continue in the pursuit of his goal. There were no excuses, and failure was not an option. He was completely committed, and he was successful as a result. Critics would say, "Arnold was just lucky that he has such good genetics." Yes, genetics are a factor, but they are not the most important factor in wining a bodybuilding competition. Arnold uses the same determination, commitment, sacrifice, and focus in all aspects of his life. As a result, he continues to live a life that is filled with enormous accomplishment.

What advantage does an Austrian with a thick accent have when trying out for movie rolls as a secret government agent? How many people told Arnold that he was "crazy" if he thought he would ever be a star? Despite enormous obstacles, Arnold has been a success at almost everything he has ever pursued.

Key #29
Advice

To get what you want, listen only to those that already have it!

I cringe when I think of all the conversations I've had with people who will start their justification of a decision with the phrase,

"I was talking with my mom about this, and…"

There is nothing wrong with Mom's advice on certain topics, but is she really a credible expert for every topic or issue? As mentioned later in this book in key#36, Mom has lots of wisdom to offer. I'm just saying that I wouldn't ask a poor person for financial advice or a couch potato for "work out" advice. I wouldn't hire a dentist to build me a house or an electrician to look at my plumbing.

> **A good mechanic always gets the right tool for the job. A successful person always gets the right advice for the topic at hand.**

I know of which I speak! Although my parents are well-meaning and love me very much, they have discouraged me from achieving most of my favorite accomplishments. If I had let them influence me negatively, here is a partial list of things that I would not have done:

- Graduated Battle School (Infantry Soldier)

- Six month UN Peacekeeping tour of Croatia (the former Yugoslavia)

- Rope Rescue team member

- Search and Rescue team member

- Rock Climbing Instructor

- Stealth Rope instructor for the RCMP

- Successfully marketed my own invention

- Got married (they thought it was too soon)

- Built and still maintain a successful business (they thought I should have kept my old sales job)

- Taught "Adult Literacy" for three years as a volunteer (thought I should get paid)

- Regularly contribute to several charities (save my money)

- Buy my dream house (thought it was over-priced)

- Speak basic greetings in several different languages (waste of energy)

- Write this book (need more credibility)

Had I listened to any of my parents' well-meaning advice, I would not have accomplished any of the above things from which I derived great enjoyment. Deciding to not follow every word of their advice wasn't disrespect but only a choice to disagree.

KEY #30
COURAGE

It takes courage to follow any of the advice in this book. It takes courage to change habits, to grow, to learn, or to walk a new path. Until you are able to find your own courage, use the courage of others (**leverage**). Knowledge and wisdom is all you need to find your courage. With self-education, you will feel your confidence grow. As your confidence grows, the possibilities will start to grow, and your life will begin to flourish.

One of the keys to finding your courage is to realize that it's okay to be uncomfortable or fearful of the unknown. Every time you move your life forward, you will be in a new place, in uncharted territory. **Every time you grow, you will again be somewhere that you've never before been. You must accept this discomfort with the unknown and get comfortable with being uncomfortable.** Once you acquire this new habit of being comfortable about being uncomfortable, you will again accelerate your rate of growth.

Confidence: revealed by a positive reaction to negative events.

- Problem-solving attitude.

- Non-defensive to criticism.

Non-confidence: revealed by negativity

- Defeatist attitude.

- Defensive to criticism.

> *"It takes a lot of courage to release the familiar and seemingly secure, to embrace the new... There is more security in the adventurous and exciting, for in movement there is life, and in change there is power."*
>
> *Alan Cohen*

> *"Courage is resistance to fear, mastery of fear—not absence of fear. Except a creature be part coward it is not a compliment to say it is brave."*
>
> *Mark Twain*

> *"Each of us is a pioneer in our own lives. We're each charting new territory every day. The people I admire are the people who willingly go forward, no matter what the odds."*
>
> *Hillary Clinton*

> *"Confidence is the hinge on the door to success."*
>
> *Mary O'Hare Dumas*

KEY #31
DESIRE

To get what you want, it helps to REALLY want it bad

Desire has a way of finding solutions. If you have a clear desire, then you will tend to see the solutions more than you will see the obstacles. The more intense your desire, the sharper your focus tends to be.

Desire coupled with the faith in yourself to attain that which you desire is a powerful force indeed.

> *"A shot glass of desire is greater than a pitcher of talent."*
>
> *Andy Munthe*

> *"A strong passion for any object will ensure success, for the desire of the end will point out the means."*
>
> *Henry Hazlitt*

> *"Decide that you want it more than you are afraid of it."*
>
> *Bill Cosby*

> *"Desire creates the power."*
>
> *Raymond Hollingwell*

> *"Desire is the key to motivation, but it's the determination and commitment to an unrelenting pursuit of your goal—a*

commitment to excellence—that will
enable you to attain the success you
seek. "

Mario Andretti

KEY #32
ACTION

All of the good intentions in the world will just sit on the shelf collecting dust without **Action.** It's not enough to simply have a goal or dream. You must put one foot in front of the other and get going toward your goals.

Actions and authentic intentions are co-dependant. Each is virtually meaningless without the other. You can do all the right things for the wrong reasons, and your result will not be what you want. You can do all the wrong things for the right reasons, and again you goal will not be realized. Doing the right things for the right reasons means that your actions are aligned with your authentic intention. When your actions and authentic intentions are in alignment, the results are certain to be positive.

Seeing your goal creates a dream—a dream of attainment. **What is far better than dreaming of achievement is remembering it. The difference between dreams and memories is action!**

By having the keys of courage and faith, there is no excuse to not act. **Acting alone does not guarantee success. However, if you fail to act, especially when opportunities** reveal themselves, your inaction is guaranteed to be rewarded with regret.

Deciding to act is deciding to avoid regret. Which you would rather have, poor results or regret? Some opportunities never come around again. You don't always have the opportunity for a second chance. If you understand how to frame "failure," then your actions will never result in regret. Regret is only possible if you fail to jump on an opportunity.

> **Opportunity will always appear to the person who is ready to jump on it. However, opportunity is content to stay hidden from the person who isn't ready to seize it.**

> *"The longest journey begins with a single step."*
> *Chinese Proverb*

> *"Ah, but a man's reach should exceed his grasp, or what's a heaven for?"*
> *Robert Browning*

KEY #33
UNDERSTANDING EXCUSES

Excuses are tools used by people to avoid responsibility for an outcome. Excuses are also a sign of insecurity and immaturity. A mature person realizes that they are responsible for how things turn out. It may not be your fault when your venture takes a wrong turn, but it is your responsibility. This gets us back to a lack of self-esteem. When you are already feeling crappy about yourself, the last thing you want to deal with is admitting that you goofed up. This same discomfort is a part of the fear of failure. You must recognize excuses for what they are and replace them with responsibility. **Excuses state that it's "someone else's fault." You can't fix other peoples faults; you can only fix your own faults.** If you want to make progress, you have to admit to yourself and all around you when you screw up, then take responsibility for the outcome. If this is a new thing for you, it will be really uncomfortable the first few times, but with consistency, it will become easier. Being successful without being responsible for your mistakes is highly unlikely. It's a matter of maturity.

CHAPTER 4
MOVING
BEYOND MEDIOCRE

KEY #34
POSSIBILITIES
(MEET ALVIN)

When you get rid of excuses, possibilities take their place.

Let me introduce you to Alvin Law. Alvin is a very talented man by anyone's standards. He has learned how to:

• Play the trombone, piano, and drums.

• Author a fantastic and inspirational book.

• Build a business that inspires tens of thousands of people a year.

• Dress himself—um, pardon?

If the last point doesn't sound impressive, you just try to button up your shirt, tie a tie, and zip up your pants without any arms. Yes that's right, without any arms. As a result of the infamous morning-sickness drug Thalidomide, Alvin was born without arms. He doesn't complain, make excuses, or ask for sympathy. He just figures out ways to deal with his challenges, and he gets the job done. Alvin embodies the military motto of **"Improvise, Adapt, and Overcome."**

During his whole life, Alvin had to endure listening to people telling him what he couldn't do. He was forever being forced to silence the doubters by doing the impossible, time and time again. Most people would have believed all of the people who always said, "You can't." Most people would have lived within the limits that were set upon them. But **Alvin understood that the only opinion that mattered in regards to his potential was his own opinion**. Alvin also understood better than most that "can't" means "won't." It was his refusal to give up and his unrelenting courage to try anything that has made his life full and plentiful in the face of adversity.

If you are the type to make excuses in life, I strongly suggest that you read *Alvin's book, Alvin's Five Laws to Overcome Anything* available at www.alvinlaw.com.

Yes, Alvin can type too. He wrote a great book, and he is a talented international speaker as well.

KEY #35
BIG POTATOES, SMALL POTATOES

As Donald Trump says, "As long as you are going to be thinking anyway, think big!" People tend to place limits on themselves based on their confidence levels. **It's impossible to achieve more than what you believe you deserve.** The more you believe is possible, the more becomes possible. This is why the first part of this book is faith. Faith in your own potential is the foundation upon which all else is built. If you think that you are small potatoes, then you are small potatoes. **All you have to do is to realize that your potatoes are as big as you are willing to grow them, and then a whole new world of possibilities will open up.**

I fully realize that the above is easier said than done, but you must first be familiar with a concept before you can start to believe it. Once you believe it, you can then start to internalize it and make it a part of who you are. Some people are able to remove the obstacles all at once and explode down a path of achievement. Most other people (myself included) need to find small successes first in order to have the courage to attempt bigger and bigger things. It's all a matter of comfort level and courage. Dr. Wayne Dyer teaches that to think big, we must first think small. Break the big goal into a bunch of smaller, less intimidating goals. Once the goal is broken down, it seems less daunting to knock off each smaller sub-goal one at a time.

Dharma plays a large role in the size of the goals we choose. If your goal is truly one that suits you, then you will naturally have more courage and energy to work towards that goal. If you are setting a goal that isn't compatible with your Dharma, then you will have less courage and energy to invest in that goal. The amount of energy you put towards a goal will determine the size of the goal. Writing this book takes an enormous amount of energy and commitment. But sharing wisdom is my Dharma, so it doesn't seem like work at all. In fact, because writing this book is a Dharma-driven endeavor, I actually receive more energy from writing than I expend.

When you hear yourself placing limitations on how much money you deserve, how happy you can be, or how far you can go in your career, just remember that the only limitations are the ones you have placed in your own path. Any obstacles that you perceive, you will be able to overcome. In the Army, I was taught to "improvise, adapt, and overcome." If there was an obstacle in my way, I would go over, under, around, or through it using any means I could. If you choose to adopt this simple problem-solving attitude, then you will be able to choose any sized goal you wish. What you don't know how to do, you will simply figure out or hire someone that can do it for you.

If you decide to build a house yourself and money is not an object, then it can be any size you choose. Many people might choose a small, simple house, since that would seem to be a more attainable goal. A small home seems more simple to build and less daunting. In actual fact, a larger house is equally attainable. You may have more to learn, but that's okay because you have the ability to learn. It may take more time, but you are only building it once! If you believe that you can build the bigger house, then you will have the courage and the energy to achieve that goal. If you don't believe you can, then the size of your house will be directly proportionate to your confidence level.

The Golden Oldies

There are hundreds of keys right under your nose

I've often heard people dismiss common, popular sayings as "fluff." This is a huge mistake. Don't let the fact that a saying is on a bumper sticker or a T-shirt trick you into dismissing it. Little blips of common wisdom aren't so little. There is valuable wisdom all around us if we would just listen and pay attention. Here are some sayings I had on the tip of my tongue, and I apologize if I have not given the proper credit for any of the following quotes. I'm sure that Zig Ziglar, Jim Rohn, or Charlie "Tremendous" Jones may be able to take credit for a couple of these.

- Obstacles are the things we see when we lose sight of our goals.

- Those who fail to prepare, prepare to fail.

- You have two ears and only one mouth—use them proportionately.

- Make hay while the sun shines.

- Do unto others as you would have them do unto you (The Golden Rule).

- Do unto others as they would have you do unto them (The Platinum Rule).

- A bird in the hand is better than two in the bush.

- Luck is a by-product of achieving a goal.

- We make our own luck.

- You can never become "above average" as long as you pursue "average" goals.

- You reap what you sow.

Blah, blah, blah, or important wisdom? There are thousands of sayings like these that have something to offer you. This wisdom is right under your nose, and you can choose to be lifted by it or you can choose to ignore it.

I can think of dozens of sayings that I have heard hundreds of times before the meaning within the saying finally hit me. I have my favorites, but they all have something to share. By being conscious of these sayings and trying to glean some wisdom from them, you will find that life just gets easier. If you focus on having a positive outlook and on growing your life, then these sayings will jump out at you. If you choose to stay negative, then you will only see negative things, and you will miss out on this wisdom.

Of course, there are other common quips that are equally unhealthy. Commonly accepted misinformation is a pet peeve of mine. Here are some examples:

- *"Money is the root of all evil"*

This is a common misquote that I've heard people often use as an excuse for their lack of ambition. It's not money, but the **want of money**, or greed, that is quoted in the

Bible as being the root of all evil. With money, you can give to charities and lift those around you. Money pays for children's hospitals, opera, and the fine arts. Money has the potential to bring a lot of good to the world. One of the greatest joys of my financial success is in my ability to give to others. If I were broke, I'd not be able to do anything other than to make ends meet. A large percentage of the profits from this book are going to charitable causes, so if there were not any book sales, there would not be any money, and these causes would not receive any benefits.

- ***"Well, that would be nice, and I'd do it if I ever won the lottery!"***

How many times have you heard this? The fact is, if you want something, you don't need the lottery to get it. People will make the "lottery statement" so that they don't have to take responsibility for their refusal to pursue or achieve their goals.

Not only can all of us live a fulfilling life, but it is our God-given right to create the opportunity to do so.

Notice that I said that it is our right to "create the opportunity," and not to simply have a fulfilling life. We have to take responsibility for taking action when opportunities present themselves; good things don't happen without a conscious effort on our part. God doesn't want us to plod through life pretending that we can only achieve our dreams if they are magically given to us by a genie in a bottle or by winning the lottery. We own our lives, and they are what we build them to be.

We can all remember being a kid and thinking that our mom was "nagging" us without just cause. As we got older, we would stumble into an experience that would prove our mom's advice to be valid and her nags to be wisdom. Isn't it funny that the older we get, the more Mom seems to make sense? As our perspective changes and as we mature, we are able to understand wisdom that was given to us a decade or more ago. Why didn't we just "get it" years ago?

How many times have you said, "If only I knew then, what I know now?" Have you ever imagined going back in time to scream sense into your younger self? I know I have. By paying attention to the wisdom around us, and by being skilled at learning from your mistakes, the process of gaining wisdom is greatly accelerated. You don't need to have the "future you" go back in time to give you valuable information. The guide in the balloon above you can already see what lies ahead and can give you what you need to know so that you don't keep making the same mistakes.

KEY #37
LEVERAGING

Leverage is the ability to produce results that are greater than your effort. You can leverage wisdom, technical knowledge, or manpower. Learning from mistakes can be leveraged as well if you choose to learn from the mistakes of others. This way, all of the time and energy that has been expended by others who have made mistakes can benefit you without any more effort than it takes to learn the lessons taught by their mistakes. Trial and error can take years if you do it yourself. You can literally gain hundreds of years of experience in a few short hours of reading. Let others fall on their faces for years on end, but not you! You know better; you know that you don't have to do things the hard way.

The reason there are so many books on success is that successful people are often generous people who want to share what they have learned for the benefit of others. Accept this generosity by paying attention to their lessons, and you will fit several lifetimes of wisdom into a few days of reading.

The "**secret to success and happiness**" **is anything but a secret**. There is a wealth of information available in almost every language, in every country in the world that will guide anyone who is seeking a path to financial and personal success.

Understanding and using the power of leverage will allow you to overcome obstacles that you would have otherwise thought impossible. Anything that you cannot do with your own power can be achieved by amplifying your power with leverage.

Key #38
What others have done before me, so can I

If others have what I want, I can have it too.

I have no idea where I learned this simple concept, but this important wisdom has always been inside me. Regardless of its origin, it is the one bit of wisdom more than any other that has given me the courage to achieve every single goal I have ever accomplished.

When I joined the Army, I had no idea of what I was getting myself into. I did not take heed upon entering; I just had the solid thought in my mind, *Tens of thousands have done this before me, so there is no way that I can't do it!* When I got to Basic Training (boot camp), there was one lesson above all others I will never forget:

> Sergeant McGee had all of us face down on the floor doing push-ups, when he heard one of the recruits say, "I can't." McGee stomped over to this recruit, got down on one knee and blasted these three words into the recruit's face, and into my mind: **"Can't means won't,** you little maggot!"

"Can't means won't"? Wow, that hit me right between the eyes like a ball-peen hammer. It was a deeply profound moment that changed the way I viewed the word "can't." It really stuck with me from that moment forward.

I was always able to do as many push-ups as that man demanded from me and that I demanded from myself.

Every time I have faced a new challenge, I have always asked the same three questions.

1. Has this been done before?

2. How can I learn to make it work?

3. Does this goal really suit me? Do I want to achieve this goal?

The statement **"What others have done before me, so can I"** is a simple and powerful one. If you think about it, it's applicable to just about any goal you can possibly imagine. If you overcome your fear of success and fear of failure, then you can state these words with confidence and go forth to achieve any reasonable goal you wish.

"Reasonable goal." Now there is a phrase that you won't often see in most books about maximizing your personal potential. I've read several books that state, **"Whatever your mind can conceive, you can achieve!"** That statement, although it has its merits, can easily be dismissed by eager skeptics as "fluff." By my estimation, this statement is only about ninety-eight percent accurate. We do have our limitations. However, our limitations are always far less significant and far fewer than we think they are. Limitations are not a negative thing at all. If you are trying to be the best at something that you have the least talent for, then you're in for a rough ride. **If you have located your talents and strive toward a goal that requires your God-given strengths, then you're bound to succeed if you just soldier on no matter what.**

I'm not saying that you should just roll over and accept your weaknesses as an inevitable burden. **Almost any weakness can be trained into a strength.** If you are chasing a serious goal, it's far less difficult if you are walking a path that complements your skill set.

KEY #39
LIMITATIONS?

Remember Alvin Law? The whole world tried to put limitations on him, and he had to prove them all wrong time after time. A piano teacher once told him that his toes were too short to ever be able to play the piano. Undaunted, Alvin knew what he wanted, and he learned how to play the piano regardless.

I would like to share with you something special to me. In 2002, I volunteered as an adult literacy tutor. We only taught our students one-on-one, so we were able to learn quite a bit about them. My first student (that I'll call Jerry) was an amazing man. He graduated high school and had made it through his first year of technical college without knowing how to read! I don't know how he did it, but he did. Without being literate, Jerry started two very successful businesses, and he had a very healthy net worth. His house was mortgage-free by the time he was thirty-five years old, and his business was doing great—and all without knowing how to read. Who would have guessed that an illiterate man could accomplish so much in life?

I met with Jerry for two hours a week, every Thursday, at a public library. He committed himself to finally learning how to read, and after only nine months, he was reading at a level that was satisfactory to him. He wasn't reading Shakespeare, but he was reading at a proficient level. When we started, he didn't even have a firm grasp of the alphabet. And now he understood both spelling and grammar to a level that allowed him to read and write.

I invite you to remember this story and the story of Alvin Law the next time you place limitations on yourself. Learning to read in your forties isn't a small task. After twelve years of being failed by the school system, it's difficult to believe you could learn to read in only nine months. Most would call it impossible, but Jerry just made it happen.

Q: "How was the dog able to climb the tree?"

A: "Nobody told him he couldn't."

Impossible?

Although most limitations are self-imposed, there are several that are imposed by the common doctrine of society. To best illustrate, I'll provide a list of some of the things that were commonly believed to be impossible:

1. Breaking the sound barrier. Chuck Yeager did it on October 14, 1947

2. The four minute mile. Was first accomplished by Roger Bannister in 1954

3. Crossing the Atlantic. No, it wasn't Columbus, he was predated by at least 200 years. The Viking ruins were found in Newfoundland to prove it.

4. Flying. Arguably, the Wright Brothers were the first to fly.

5. Going around the world in eighty days.

6. End to the slave trade.

7. Nuclear power.

8. The light bulb.

9. Electricity.

10. An affordable lap top computer.

11. Cell phones.

12. Women voting.

13. The world being round.

14. The sun is at the center of our system.

15. Space flight.

16. The automobile.

17. European Union.

18. Climbing Mount Everest. Over 500 summiteers in 2007 alone.

Every one of the above points was believed to be impossible. Each of the above topics had scores of critics laughing at anyone who thought these goals to be possible. Every single one of the above accomplishments happened despite the popular opinion, not because of it.

The next time someone laughs at your goals or dreams, try to realize that the criticism may be evidence that you are onto something good!

KEY #40
MENTORSHIP

I have a great many mentors, but very few of them have a clue that I consider them to be a mentor. I tend to consider both the strengths and weaknesses of each person I know so each person I meet becomes a teacher. As a result of putting forth effort into seeing people's strengths; they are often clear to me. The reason I look for the good in people is so I can better understand myself and grow from what I draw from others. Everyone has a quality worth admiring, so if you notice yourself admiring a quality in someone, it should beg the question: **"If I admire this quality, should I not try to adopt this quality into my own life?"**

I'd like to share with you a story of my friend's father. To me, it's an amazing story that has taught me that anything is possible if you are willing to do the work to make it happen.

The wealthy mailman

Fred was a mailman for over thirty-five years. As a mailman, he never received a large salary, but what he earned was enough to keep food on the table for his wife and four children. His kids didn't have the fancier things in life, but none of them ever felt as though they went without. Some people would look at a man who carried a mailbag for so many years and assume that he was a man who lacked ambition in life. They would be wrong!

The critics would be wrong for two main reasons:

1. Fred truly enjoyed his work. Few people are blessed with a job they actually enjoy. Most of us trudge through life hating our occupation, but not Fred.

2. Fred had a life outside work that was full and rich with accomplishments.

Don't ever let your job define who you are. It is common for someone to say, "I'm only a mailman," when what they should be thinking and saying is, "I'm a champion who happens to deliver the mail so that I can pay my bills." Do you see the difference? **Our occupation is just something we do to generate an income, nothing more. Don't let it define who you are or limit your**

potential. If anything, your potential should define your occupation.

Now let me share with you the wonderful story of Fred, not the mailman, but **Fred the dream builder!**

> When Fred was a young man with a young family, he found that he was restless. His family was provided for, but there was something deep down inside picking at him that he just couldn't ignore. Although he had a very ordinary income, he imagined what it would be like to provide an extraordinary life for his family. With this restlessness, a dream started to form. He didn't know exactly what he was seeking; he only knew that he wanted more for his family. Driven by this nagging feeling of wanting more, Fred started to pay attention to potential opportunities.
>
> One way to see opportunities is to do an inventory of assets. Fred started thinking about his work schedule, and he realized that he had the greatest asset of all: lots of free time. Fred's mail route started early in the morning, and he was finished by 2:30 p.m. every day. He knew that if an opportunity arose, that at least he would have the time to pursue it. All he needed now was the opportunity.

Opportunity will always appear to the person who is ready to jump on it. However, opportunity is content to stay

hidden from the person who isn't ready to seize it.

One afternoon after work, Fred was enjoying a piping hot coffee, softened by a dash of evaporated milk. The sections of his newspaper were pulled apart and neatly restacked on the table. As he was casually flipping through the classifieds, an advertisement in the Real Estate section caught his eye. A Realtor was advertising a twenty-acre parcel just one hour from the city. Something about this ad started the dream wheels turning for Fred, and he knew that he had to take a look. A good buddy of his was a Realtor, so he called up his friend and arranged to see this property. Fred knew he couldn't afford to purchase this land on his own, so he asked his brother to go in with him. When he got to the land, he started to see the potential it offered. He was so excited about this parcel that his enthusiasm soon won over his brother, and they agreed to buy it together.

Fred the **dream builder** had taken the first step. He saw an opportunity, and he found a way to pounce on it. Buying the land was just the first step. Unless he wanted to pitch a tent and just have a twenty-acre campground for his family, he had to find a way to build a cabin. As a mailman, Fred had limited financial resources. But what he did have was time.

On Fred's mail route, he noticed that there were a few houses that were beyond repair and needed to be torn down. It occurred to him that the building material in those homes could be recycled. Then the light bulb lit up! He immediately went to the city with the addresses of these homes, and he found out who the owners were. Fred contacted the owners, and he offered to demolish the homes for free, providing that he was given a long time-line to do so. Also, he was allowed to salvage all of the building materials. The homeowners gladly agreed, and Fred got to work.

Fred and his oldest children would pry off each board carefully, pull the nails, and stack the wood in his trailer. He would then straighten and save all of the nails in coffee tins. Once the trailer was loaded, he would haul the material to his twenty acres and store it. As you can well imagine, this was a lot of work. But for Fred, recycling was a labor of love.

Over time, Fred was able to accumulate enough free recycled material to build not only his cabin, but three other cabins, two huge garages, three out-houses, one root cellar, one gazebo, one baseball diamond, and a fifty-foot bridge. Bonaire Acres is the name of this amazing place, and my wife and I love being invited for an occasional overnight stay. Every time we visit, I am reminded of the power of a dream. **With focus, hard** work, and determination, almost anything is possible. Fred is certainly one of my most powerful mentors, and he didn't even know it until I gave him a copy of this book.

KEY #41
MODELING

Modeling is the next step after mentoring. As Anthony Robbins wrote:

> **"Modeling is the pathway to excellence. The movers and shakers of the world are often professional modelers—people who have mastered the art of learning everything they can by following other people's experience, rather than their own."**

This concept is a simple one. Just think of someone who has something that you want. Figure out what that person did to get that thing, and then do the same thing he did to get it! Do you remember the title of **Key # 38**? **What others have done before me, so can I.**

- **Mentoring is the act of acknowledging and respecting the positive traits of others.**

- **Modeling is the act of doing what your mentors are doing to achieve a desired result.**

Modeling provides a huge amount of **leverage**. As Tony Robbins says, use other people's experience rather than your own. Both the positive and negative results produced by others have valuable lessons to teach.

Modeling Got Me through College

I was terrified of college. I had been out of high school for six years, and I didn't have a successful academic track record at all. I coasted through high school just doing the bare minimum required to graduate. At the time, I wasn't interested in school, so I didn't bother putting any effort into it. By the time I enrolled in college at the age of twenty-six, my attitude toward school had improved greatly. I was more mature and very curious about the world around me. Also, college wasn't free, so I knew I had to do well, but I had no idea of how to achieve in college.

When class started, it didn't take long to realize who the class clowns and class achievers were. All I simply did was start hanging around with the top students and whatever they did, I did. If that group was studying, I was studying with them while the class clowns were goofing off. I had been the class clown in high school, so I knew from experience that those actions would produce poor results. Poor results were simply not acceptable to me in college. As it turned out, I graduated, and with great marks as well.

Modeling is a powerful and transferable tool that can be utilized for any goal. With just this single key, you will be amazed at what you can accomplish.

Key #42
Why not you?

If other people have the things you want, then why not you? If you know of someone who is driving your dream car, why are you just dreaming about that car? Do you believe that the person driving your dream car is just "lucky"? Do you believe that only doctors, lawyers, and lottery winners can drive nice cars? **The fact is that anyone who has the desire to achieve their financial goals can drive their dream car.** Nobody is going to give it to you for free. However, by the same token, nobody can stop you from achieving it either. **The only person who can stop you from achieving your goals is YOU.** When a critic asks you, "What makes you think that you can?" simply answer, "What makes you think I can't?!" With the tools, or keys, that you have already acquired to this point, it should be clear to you that there is no reason at all why you can't have the life and things you desire.

> **Greatness can come from any background. It's not where you are that matters, but where you are going.**

Let me share with you the story of my first year in my current business. In my first year I only grossed about $25,000. After expenses, I probably only kept about half of that before taxes. I wasn't exactly making my fortune yet, but I wasn't concerned. I knew where I was going and what waited for me down the road. Image is an important factor in my current business. I deal with clients who put a lot of trust and faith in my abilities. The way I dress and the car I drive are interpreted as reflections of my competence level.

Unfortunately for me, I couldn't afford a decent car in my first year. Actually, this is an understatement—the car I was driving was fifteen years old with 355,000 kms (220,587 miles) on it. The paint was peeling off the hood, and the motor barely ran. It sounded a bit like the Disney car, Chitty Chitty Bang Bang. I actually used to park it down the road from clients' homes so they couldn't see what I was driving. I'm certain that car lost me several clients based on the image it presented. My wife felt awful for me, but I never complained. I was just grateful that I had a car at all. I was actually happy that my first car was a junker because I knew that when I was successful that old car would make for a good story.

In my second year, I bought a much better car. But in my third year, I bought the dream car, a gorgeous Jaguar S-type. If I had been able to buy the Jag the first year, I just wouldn't have appreciated it as much. I prefer the feeling of accomplishment derived from traveling a difficult road over that of an easy road. This is why I'm not intimidated by the size of a goal. I'm simply prepared to do the work that is required regardless of how difficult it is.

If you are in a poor financial situation then you are likely surrounded by people that are in the same situation. If you realize that you are capable of changing your position in life, then you will be able to take the action required to do so. Don't let your history or your current position in life discourage you from pursuing your goals and dreams. The deeper you feel that you are in a hole, the further it is to climb out of it—but you can still climb out of it! No hole is too deep, no mountain is too high. Just take the first step and repeat that step as many times as necessary. If you do the work, your position will improve, but if you don't, it won't. **What others have done before you, so can you!**

KEY #43
YOU ARE A PRODUCT
OF YOUR ENVIRONMENT

You have likely heard a variation of the statement, **"If you want to fly with the eagles, then don't hang around with the turkeys."** I remember years ago, my uncle Bruce commented on a troubled youth: **"Until that kid stops hanging around with bums, he's doomed to end up as a bum."** That kid never did change the crowd he hung around with, and whataya know—he was doomed to a life filled with drugs and jail time.

Anyone who has worked with criminals will tell you that the only criminals that don't repeat offend are the ones that have changed their peer group. If they get out of jail and jump right back into the same group of friends, then it is just a matter of time before they re-offend, get caught, and go back to jail. This works both ways; the people you surround yourself with will either lift you or sink you.

Making and maintaining a friendship requires effort. So once you have accepted the fact that your friends influence your success, you must then make the hard choice of which relationships to foster and which relationships you should let falter. **All that you have to do is to stop putting effort into people who are dragging you down and redirect that effort into people who will lift you up.**

I realize that this notion will stir emotion. We care about our friends, and nobody likes being told with whom they should hang around. However, carefully choosing your peer group is a necessary move on your path to growth. You have to be around people that encourage you to be happy—not people who tell you all of the reasons you can't be happy. You need support from those who tell you that you **CAN,** not poison from "friends" who tell you that you can't. The choice is that of inhabiting either a positive (constructive) or negative (destructive) environment.

Meet "like minded" people. Choose your peer group carefully. Choose people who either have what they want or people who are determined to get it for themselves. Networking is a topic that has several books dedicated to it. One major guru of networking is Dr. Ivan Misner. Dr. Misner is the founder of BNI, the world's largest business networking organization. He has authored and co-authored several books on the topic that are worthwhile reads. If you don't know the people you would like to, there are books out there that can teach you how to meet them. Dale Carnegie's famous *How to Win Friends and Influence People* is one of these books.

Most people have mediocre goals, and consequently they get mediocre results. If you want to be like most people then keep hanging around with most people.

> **You can choose to run with the ordinary majority, or you can run with the extraordinary few who actually get what they want out of life. The path less traveled is the only path for successful people. If you don't march to the beat of your own drum, you will be a slave to some other drummer.**

CHAPTER 5
THE WISDOM TO
MAXIMIZE YOUR
POTENTIAL

KEY #44
GIVERS GAIN®

Sometimes what you want, needs to come from others. You will need to be the type of person they want to give to.

Financial gain is neither the main focus nor motivator for this book. However, **financial gain is simply a natural result of unlocking your life and releasing your potential.** What is far more important than financial gain is personal gain. When you are on your deathbed, you won't care much about the size of your bank account, but you will care about the legacy of good times and warm memories you are leaving behind.

Have you ever been to a funeral service where people talk about the dead guy's huge house or fancy car? Of course not. All that people will remember is the type of person you were. Either you were respected or you were not. In the end, all that we have is respect.

Respect for others is something that is getting harder to find in our society. People are becoming more and more self-absorbed and less caring about the needs of others.

- Have you ever pulled over to the side of the road to help someone change a flat tire?

- Have you shoveled the snow off of your neighbor's sidewalk?

- Have you ever mowed a senior citizen's lawn for them?

- Have you ever moved out of your bus seat, to allow an elderly person or a pregnant lady to rest?

If you can't answer "yes" to any of these things or similar questions, you have to ask yourself why that is? It's not because you're a bad person, it's because you aren't thinking beyond your own needs.

Generosity and self-respect are linked. **When one respects oneself, one is able to respect others.** When you feel good about yourself and respect yourself, you will naturally have the urge to give to others. One way of gaining respect is by being generous. When you start to give your time to others, people will look at you with respect and afford you dignity. When you consistently receive respect as a result of your generosity, you can't help but to start to feel pride in yourself. You will find that you will gain far more than you give. This is the natural cycle of things. Giving starts the receiving process.

Maslow's pyramid chart illustrates that the highest functioning human is one who has all of her personal needs already met and so is able and driven to provide for the needs of others.

Do you remember the **Golden Oldies Key**? One of the biggest "golden oldies" is the Golden Rule: **"Do unto others as you would have them do unto you."** Doesn't this make just a little more sense now? Could it be that this old Bible saying was trying to teach this concept? It's best if you give just for the sake of giving. However, if you need a reason, then just try to understand the universal truth: that **Givers Gain**® (BNI Corporate Motto). There is another version of this that I prefer, known as the Platinum Rule; **"Do unto others as they would have you do unto them."** This way you will give what **they** want to receive, not what **you** would want to receive.

Givers Gain® is also true with the giving of respect. **If you take the time to treat even the lowliest person with dignity and respect, you will be worthy of the respect of the entire world.** If you are the type of person who belittles others and picks on those weaker than you, then you have no hope of ever gaining any real respect or dignity.

Here is a personal example of how Givers Gain®:

> I'm a Canadian, so my winters involve lots of snow shoveling. The first snowfall of 2006 gave us a four-inch layer of the heavy white stuff, so out came the snow shovel for my cold-weather workout.

When I was done with my walkway, I felt ambitious, so I also shoveled the walk for the neighbors on each side of me. It was no big deal; I just wanted to work up a bit of a sweat, and this was the easiest way for me to do that.

That evening, the snow started again, so I made a mental note to get up early enough that I could shovel the walk before going to work. When morning came, I looked out my window to see how much snow had fallen, and to my surprise, my walk was already shoveled! My neighbor had decided to re-pay me by clearing off my walk. This started a friendly, fun competition. We started racing outside during each snowfall to shovel the other person's walk before they could shovel ours. The neighbor on the other side of me soon joined in the game and started shoveling not only my walk but also the walk on the other side of him as well. There was one week where I was away on business with my pregnant wife left home alone. During that week, it snowed almost every day, but my wife didn't have to shovel even once. Without being asked, the neighbors were more than happy to cover for me while I was away. **Givers Gain**®.

This same principle works in any situation where you have an opportunity to give a little of your time to others. When people see you making an effort to help others, your deeds do not go unnoticed. You will reap what you sow.

KEY #45
INTENTION

We judge ourselves based on our intentions; others judge us based on our actions.

Let me tell you about Bob. Bob is a fellow with great intentions and a big heart, but the rubber never seems to meet the road. What I mean is, Bob talks a good game, but he never actually gets anything done. If you need a favor, he's never there for you. He loves having others do his work for him, but he won't lift a finger to help others. He'll lend you money, because it doesn't involve effort, but he won't show up on moving day to lift a sofa. Bob will defend his laziness by saying, "Yeah, but I have a good heart!" Well, sorry Bob, but a good heart doesn't pay the bills, fix the car, do the dishes, or maintain a friendship. Just having good intentions isn't enough. **It is our actions, and the results that our actions produce, that define who we are.** If you expect others to respect you, you must be aware that you will only receive the amount of respect you command. You can only command respect through consistent positive actions throughout your life. Likewise, you must be a big enough person to give respect to others. **Small people rarely give compliments, but they are always eager to receive them.**

It's what is in your heart when you act, not your actions alone, that are the measure of your good. Do the right thing for the right reasons.

There is a lesson shared in the Bible's New Testament that states: **"The man who stands in public praising God so that others will notice will receive his rewards; however, his rewards will be no greater than that of the man who worships privately at home."** There are also several lessons that state: **"You may fool others, but you can't fool God, for He knows what is truly in your heart."**

Thoughts on Intention:

> **Doing the right thing to gain favor is a transparent act that fools no one. Doing the right thing out of a desire to give, teach, or help is not always an obvious act, nor is it always rewarded; it is, however, the only true way to act and to be genuine in your actions.**

> **It is not your intentions that will result in reward, only your actions.**

KEY #46
EVERYONE MAKES AN IMPACT

What you choose to do or not do with your life has an enormous effect on the world around you. This is relevant to understanding the power that is within us all. To help you to understand the power of your actions, here is a story that literally made me cry the first few times that I read it.

I hope that you enjoy it. More importantly, I hope that you understand its relevance to your own life.

57 CENTS...(source unknown)

A sobbing little girl stood near a small church from which she had been turned away because it was *too crowded*. "I can't go to Sunday School," she sobbed to the pastor as he walked by.

Seeing her shabby, unkempt appearance, the pastor guessed the real reason she had been turned away. He took her by the hand, took her inside, and found a place for her in the Sunday School class. The child was so happy they had found room for her, and she went to bed that night thinking of the children who have no place to worship Jesus.

Some two years later, this child lay dead in one of the poor tenement buildings. The parents called for the kindhearted pastor who had befriended their daughter to handle the final arrangements. As her poor little body was being moved, a worn and crumpled purse was found that seemed to have been rummaged from some trash dump. Inside was found 57 cents and a note scribbled in childish handwriting: "This is to help build the little church bigger so more children can go to Sunday School." For two years she had saved for this offering of love.

When the pastor tearfully read that note, he knew instantly what he would do. Carrying this note and the cracked, red pocketbook to the pulpit, he told the story of her unselfish love and devotion. He challenged his deacons to get busy and raise enough money for the larger building.

But the story does not end there. A newspaper learned of the story and published it. It was read by a Realtor™ who offered them a parcel of land worth many thousands. When told that the church could not pay so much, he offered it for 57 cents.

Church members made large donations. Checks came from far and wide. Within five years, the little girl's gift had increased to $250,000—a huge sum for that time (the early 1900's). Her unselfish love had paid an enormous dividend.

When you are in the city of Philadelphia, look up the Temple Baptist Church, with a seating capacity of 3,300, and Temple University where hundreds of students are trained. Have a look, too, at the Good Samaritan Hospital and at a Sunday School building that houses hundreds of Sunday school children, so that no child in the area will ever need to be left outside during Sunday school time.

In one of the rooms of this building may be seen the picture of the sweet face of the little girl whose 57 cents, so sacrificially saved, made such remarkable history. Alongside it is a portrait of the kind pastor, Dr. Russell H. Conwell, author of the book, Acres of Diamonds.

This story is a wonderful example of the ripple effect that our actions can have. By understanding the power of your actions, you will be more likely to choose them carefully.

Go ahead. Grab a tissue and a glass of water. This story brought a tear to my eye, so I just had to find a way to include this story in this book.

> *"You may never know what results come from your actions;*
> *But if you do nothing, there will be no results."*
>
> *Gandhi*

Ask yourself this: "What type of person do I want to be?" Do you want to just improve your own life, or is it important for you to lift others as well? Once you make this decision, you will be more conscious of each decision you make. The effect or lack of effect that your actions have on others may be immeasurable.

KEY #47
DON'T ARGUE: YOU SHOULDN'T HAVE TO BE RIGHT

Here is one key that was hugely important for me to understand. I used to argue with anyone—about anything. I just couldn't tolerate an opinion that differed from my own. This stemmed from a belief that, if my opinion mattered, then I would matter. For me to be right, there had to be something right about me. If I could get someone to agree with my point of view, I would feel important and influential. By convincing someone else, I felt that I was smarter than they, and it just took some arguing to prove it! Once I realized that it wasn't about me and that my opinions were not weakened by contradictory opinions, I was then able to let go of a lot of anger. Getting angry at the opinion of others is a sure sign of insecurity. Other people's opinions are a product of who they are, so if I can't accept their opinions, then I can't accept them for who they are. We all have a right to believe anything we want to believe, regardless of what we believe is right or wrong.

It is possible to respect an opinion without agreeing with it. For instance, you don't have to agree with, or support, homosexuality to respect homosexuals. (I chose this topic as it often evokes emotion in people.) The fact that I happen to be a heterosexual isn't affected in any way by shaking the hand of a man who is gay. His beliefs or orientation aren't going to make me any less heterosexual just because I'm not angry with him. Of course, homosexuality is not a belief system. However, the point remains the same. Differences need to be respected. This concept is transferable to any differences, whether it is differences in beliefs, lifestyle, culture, or physical appearance. We don't have to agree with or condone the differences in order to respect the rights of others to be different.

Opinions can be contagious, but there is no need to avoid being exposed to opinions or ideas that contradict our own. Opinions should never be considered to be a threat *unless they are highly negative or filled with hate.* Religious wars have been and are now being fought for the sake of being "right." Believe in what you like and believe it as strongly as you like; just don't battle, or go to war to protect your beliefs. It is people's actions that create a threat—not their beliefs.

Let others believe what they wish. If you want your beliefs to be respected, you must also respect the beliefs of others, regardless of how silly or wrong you may think they are. You may go to war to protect your family, human rights, way of life, or sovereignty—but don't go just because someone has a different belief system from yours.

If you are secure in what you believe, then there should never be cause to feel threatened by contradictory beliefs. If you believe that the entire universe was created in six days, then there is no need to attack those who believe that it took billions of years to create the heavens and earth.

The truth is independent of our beliefs.

When the scientific community (the Church) believed that the world was flat, this belief was touted as an absolute fact. Anyone who said anything different (Galileo) was jailed or put to death as a heretic. Dissent equaled treason against the Church. No matter how strongly the people believed that the world was flat, the world didn't get any flatter. It didn't matter how many people were punished for saying the world was round, the world still didn't get any flatter. The truth was and is that the world was and is a sphere. The truth wasn't affected by the so-called "facts" of the day. The truth is independent of what we believe. By understanding that we really don't "know" much (if anything), we will then have the wisdom to take both new and old information with a grain of salt.

> *"The only true wisdom is in knowing that we know nothing."*
>
> **Socrates**

When people are confronted with an opinion that is way out of their comfort zone, they are quick to call others "crazy" for having that opinion. If an opinion is out of your comfort zone, it doesn't matter how true it is; you will find difficulty accepting it as truth. Just because something sounds "crazy" doesn't mean that it's not true.

Imagine a UFO lands in your own back yard; an alien emerges from the craft, has a nice chat and cup of coffee with you, and then flies away. If it happened, it happened, and there is no amount of denial that's going to change that. However, you will still be called a "crazy nut job" by most anyone to whom you tell the story.

You could have a home video, still photos, and even a lock of hair from the alien, and it still wouldn't matter. A few more people might be convinced, but the majority will ignore the truth and find ways to discredit your evidence. The easiest way to trivialize and discredit a story is to label it as "crazy."

It takes maturity and self-confidence to be open to uncomfortable possibilities. For most people, making a lot of money is a very uncomfortable possibility. **The idea that you are capable of far more than you ever thought possible is a very uncomfortable possibility, but it's true regardless of how uncomfortable you feel about it.** The more open you are to the possibility that some of your beliefs might be self-limiting, the more able you will be to identify and remove those beliefs. Also, if you are able to accept the possibility that you might not be "right," then you will have the ability to have much more respect for the uncomfortable opinions and beliefs of others. Just because something is uncomfortable to you, doesn't mean that it isn't correct.

The stronger you hold onto the idea that others should agree with you, the smaller your world will be.

It's important to get comfortable with being uncomfortable. **To learn anything, it means that you will have to accept that there is more for you to learn.** Anytime we try something new, it is going to be uncomfortable since we haven't done it before. If you're not able to deal with the discomfort, then you will not be able to grow. Building your muscles works the same way. If you want to build your muscles and increase your strength, then you must push yourself well past a level that is comfortable. If you don't go beyond what is comfortable, your muscles will not grow in either size or strength.

> *"Confidence comes not from always being right, but from not fearing to be wrong."*
>
> *Peter T. McIntyre*

KEY #48
IGNORANCE/ARROGANCE VS. CONFIDENCE/WISDOM

This is an example of positive versus negative traits and positive versus negative results. Remember that choosing positive energy is constructive, and negative energy is destructive.

Confidence is sometimes mistaken for arrogance. At a glance, there seems to be a fine line between confidence and arrogance, but in fact they are drastically different things.

- Arrogance stems from a lack of confidence, not over-confidence.

- Arrogance manifests when a person doesn't believe in themselves, so they run around with their nose in the air trying to convince themselves and others that they are better than those around them.

- Arrogance begs for the respect of others.

- Arrogance is blind to any truth that threatens its own beliefs.

- Arrogance needs to be validated by others.

- Arrogance needs to hear that it is right, and you are wrong.

- Confidence stems from strength, maturity, and wisdom.

- Confidence occurs when people have faith in their own abilities.

- Confidence is quiet and doesn't have to show off to others.

- Confidence doesn't require attention or affirmation from others.

- Confidence is wise and able to accept the truth, regardless of what the truth reveals.

- Confidence doesn't have to be validated by others.

- Confidence doesn't insist that it is correct and that you are not.

It is important to understand the difference between confidence and arrogance so you can identify these traits in yourself and choose to accept or adjust these traits. Also, when you are able to recognize the difference in others, you will find you have more patience for arrogance since you will realize that the arrogant person is actually crying out for help.

> *"Every obnoxious act is a cry for help."*
>   *Zig Ziglar*

Confidence is the ability to jump into a situation with little idea of what you are doing, but having faith in yourself to figure it out.

Bravery is having no idea what you are getting into—no idea if you can make it work, but you know it has to be done. You make it your responsibility to do it. Bravery is acting in spite of your fears.

Arrogance is telling others how it should be done—taking credit for the positive, and blaming others for the negative.

We choose what we wish to be. If you wouldn't choose to put a particular character trait in your resume or on

your business card, then why would you choose to keep it in your personality?

KEY #49
FORGIVE YOURSELF, AND OTHERS

To fully release your potential, you must fully release any excess baggage that may be weighing you down.

When is the last time you screwed up badly? Did you lose sleep over it or beat yourself up about it? Did you ask yourself, "How could I be so stupid?" I can certainly think of a few times when I put my foot in my mouth by blurting out something ridiculous. I can even remember times when my screw-ups caused harm to my reputation. These things happen to all of us from time to time; none of us is perfect.

It is not a positive use of our energy to spend time worrying about the consequences of our mistakes. What is a positive use of our energy is to accept responsibility for our mistakes. If you are able to correct the wrong, then of course correct it. However, we are often not able to correct the wrong. In this case, the only thing left to do is to learn from the wrong so that it will not be repeated in the future. We can't change the past; we can only learn and grow from the lessons that our mistakes teach us. By forgiving yourself for being an imperfect human being, you will then be able to release yourself from the baggage of regret. Regrets weigh heavily on the mind, so the more you can dump the regrets from your mind, the freer your mind will be.

> **Accepting responsibility for our mistakes doesn't mean that we are deciding to punish ourselves for them; it means that we are ready to learn and grow from them.**

When was the last time someone did something nasty to you? Did you lose sleep over that, too? Do you spend time wishing for either revenge or justice of some sort? What about the last time someone did something nasty to someone else that resulted in you losing sleep? Did you wallow in the question, "How could you have done such a thing?"

Why is it that we choose to punish ourselves for the negative actions of others? By spending your time and energy being angry at the person who did something wrong, you are punishing yourself by focusing on the negative energy of the misdeed. What is needed is to forgive the person for their wrongdoing. Forgiving doesn't mean that there won't be or shouldn't be any consequences, it just means that you won't be hurting yourself by hating the wrong doer.

> *By forgiving, you are not letting the wrongdoer off the hook; you are letting yourself off the hook.*

"Bitterness is like drinking a cup of poison and expecting someone else to die."

unknown

"Please forgive me for my trespasses, as I forgive those who trespass against me."

The Lord's Prayer

KEY #50
SKEPTICS SHOULDN'T HAVE AIRTIME

As we have already learned, choosing the positive is choosing to be constructive with your life, and choosing the negative is destructive to your life.

Skepticism is usually a negative use of one's energy. Thus, it should not have too much focus placed on it. **The opposite of skepticism is curiosity.** When you are exposed to information that seems unlikely or uncomfortable, the immature reaction is immediate skepticism. The mature reaction is immediate curiosity. Both reactions shield you from being gullible or being suckered into believing false information. The skeptics will not have the perspective to see any truth that may be right in front of them. Their skepticism (being negative) is blinding the skeptic from any possible truth.

The curious, however, are equally open to either outcome, true or false. The curious are not concerned with how comfortable the truth is but only about what appears to be the truth of the matter.

The mainstream media sources have a habit of giving more airtime to skeptics than to curious investigative reporters. As a result, the bulk of the population is only familiar with the skeptical viewpoints, and thus any information that contradicts the skeptics is treated as silly or trivial. People have a natural tendency to avoid skepticism and criticism. Most people, therefore, will simply go along with the skeptics to avoid being ridiculed or criticized.

A major change I would like to see in society is for skeptics to be the ones who are trivialized and marginalized. It is the curious investigators who should be given the majority of airtime in the media, thus receiving the majority of the focus from the bulk of the population. By replacing the immense amount of negative energy put into skepticism with the positive energy of curiosity, there would be a powerful surge in the progress of the human race.

Imagine if our scientists were not concerned with being laughed at by their peers, but instead were empowered to ask any question about any topic they chose. Imagine what would happen if we were curious about alternative energy instead of constantly being skeptical about the viability of solar, wind, and geothermal energy. If the immature skeptics were trivialized instead of the mature curious, then there would be solar panels on the roof of every home on earth. The reduction in fossil fuel dependency would be astronomical; thus, the demand for fossil-fuel-generated electricity would be enormously reduced. The only thing stopping this from happening is the misinformation of the skeptics who are treated as experts.

In Europe, it is very common to have solar panels on homes to augment electricity; yet in North America, it is exceedingly rare. The difference is public consciousness. It's what is believed to be normal or abnormal that has people following a trend. Few people are willing to put up with the skeptics who constantly criticize what they don't understand, so instead they simply go with the flow and conform to what the skeptics tell them is normal and acceptable.

What a different world we would have if we didn't just accept that the world is flat to avoid being ridiculed for our curiosity. The world stayed flat for more than 200 years after Galileo. **What progress could we have made if the skeptics were treated as children, and the curious as mature adults?** Our society's values are backwards in this regard. Skepticism retards the evolution of the human race.

If this one societal change were to occur, then all who control the media and even our politicians would be completely disempowered to misdirect the truth any longer. In the media, they provide the news they think will sell. If society changed from seeking skepticism to seeking curiosity, then the media would respond to the new market demands.

By changing all journalism into investigative journalism, the world would be flipped on its head for the better. The progress of the human race would instantly be launched into a quantum leap of social evolution.

Skepticism is a highly effective tool that is used to combat the curious. The curious are often trivialized and marginalized by calling them "conspiracy theorists." When the tobacco industry was first questioned about the health risks of their products, they quickly reacted with skeptical self-published studies. The tobacco companies ran a public misinformation campaign of skepticism that trivialized anyone who was foolish enough to even suggest that tobacco had potential health hazards.

The tobacco companies knew the power of skepticism, and they used it to their advantage for decades before they finally lost their stranglehold on the public consciousness. Even with all of the evidence, there are still people today who are swayed by the decades-old arguments, and they are skeptical of the fact that tobacco use poses health risks.

By being aware of the tactics of those who use skepticism to combat the curious, we can then free ourselves to make up our own minds about what is and what isn't true. We fear being thought of as gullible, so we follow the popular skeptics. What an irony it is that skepticism is used to avoid being caught as gullible, yet it is curiosity that actually protects us from being gullible. We swallow a skeptic's story far easier than a "crazy" story of curiosity.

KEY #51
DON'T STEP ON FINGERS
(THEY MAY BE ATTACHED TO
A FUTURE HELPING HAND)

Any dishonest or negative action that you take against another person will be noticed. In business, I've seen people who regularly bash the competition as a tactic for raising their own profiles. What these people don't seem to understand is that being friendly to the competition will elevate you by showing that you are not afraid of your competitors. By complimenting your competition, you are actually strengthening your image, not weakening it. Transversely, of course, trying to strengthen your image by bashing others does nothing but weaken your position.

If you live with integrity, then you will never choose to step on someone else's toes to get ahead. Living with integrity means that, given the choice, you would rather put another in front of you than to shove him out of the way so that you can be out in front. If you are worthy of advancement, the advancement will naturally occur on its own as long as you take the positive actions required to move forward. There will never be any benefit in hiding the talent of others so that yours will shine the brightest. **If there is another more talented than yourself, then it would be better to lift him up in any way you can than to push his head under the water.** You actions will be recognized, and your integrity will not go unnoticed. Of course, you are choosing to do the right thing because it is correct and not just for the recognition of others.

Living with integrity is doing the right thing because it's right regardless of the results or recognition. **By keeping yourself on the right track, you will keep yourself immersed in wonderful, positive energy. By choosing the wrong track, you will be dunking your head into a pool of putrid negative energy.** Choosing the wrong way to go is choosing a path to certain self-assassination. You may be satisfied with the temporary results, but in the long run you will always lose.

KEY #52
GRATITUDE: THE ONLY PATH TO TRUE SUCCESS

Gratitude is a key that provides a deeper and more meaningful understanding for many of the other keys. Happiness can not be attained without gratitude, and if we aren't happy then what is the point? Without gratitude, you will always be thirsty for more and never be able to enjoy what you already have.

In some extreme situations, gratitude can seem difficult. For example, a very good friend of mine was diagnosed with a rare form of leukemia. Instead of feeling angry about getting leukemia at the age of fifty-six, he instead decided to feel grateful for not getting leukemia at the age of thirty. If he had been diagnosed at the age of thirty, he would have been grateful that it didn't happen when he was twenty.

My friend is grateful for the life that he has enjoyed up to this point, not woeful that his life will be cut shorter than he expected. **He's happy for what he has, not sad about what he doesn't have.**

> *"It's not having what you want; it's wanting what you've got."*
> **Sheryl Crow**

I had open-heart surgery when I was twenty-nine years old. If you have ever had your chest cracked open, you'll know that it's not a lot of fun. I could have felt sorry for myself for having to deal with such a thing at such a young age. But, instead of lamenting my situation, I decided to be grateful. I had quite a lot to be grateful for:

- The fact that I survived long enough to get the surgery.

- The rare type of operation I had allowed me to not be dependant on blood thinners the rest of my life.

- The operation provided me with more energy than I was used to having.

- I was able to re-evaluate my career path. Prior to the surgery, I wanted to be a police officer. With that no longer an option, I chose a much more suitable path.

- Being a Canadian, I didn't have to pay a dime for the surgery! They even paid for my accommodations and flight to the only hospital in the country that could handle that type of surgery.

There is always a lot to be grateful for if you have the perspective to see it. Being grateful is a very positive use of your energy, whereas feeling like a victim is a negative drain on your energy.

Do you remember the story of Fred the dream builder? It was Fred's gratitude for what he had that allowed him to be a great man and provide a great life for his family. Fred never wished to live in a 10,000 square foot mansion, so he never felt as though he missed out on anything. Instead of being envious of others, he was grateful for what he had. The attitude of gratitude is the key to feeling good about your life and yourself.

What would you suppose that Alvin Law, a man born without arms, is grateful for? I'd say that Alvin is pretty darn grateful for the fact that he has two good legs and ten good toes! Those legs and toes have allowed him to accomplish great things, and you can bet that he takes good care of them. Any energy that Alvin could have spent feeling sorry for himself for being different would have detracted from his love of life. **Alvin's gratitude for his abilities has allowed him to enjoy and savor his life.**

Let us use the ugly example of divorce to illustrate the power of gratitude. Divorce is usually a nasty and difficult process for everyone involved. Both spouses, the kids, in-laws, and even the friends of the couple can be affected by the divorce. It isn't difficult to allow a negative time in your life such as divorce to be a significant drain on your energy and/or self esteem.

Here are some useful tools to help deal with the regret that often accompanies divorce. Try to recognize that:

1. You have done your best to be the best spouse that you could.

2. You have done your best to seek help for yourself and the marriage.

3. The longer you stay with the wrong person, the further away you will be from right person.

The next step is to find a place for gratitude. What is the upside of all this? Try to remember that the time spent with that person was not a waste of time. All of the negative experiences had something useful to teach.

1. Remember the good times and be grateful for them.

2. Be grateful that you are strong enough to end the negative relationship now and not ten years from now. What's worse than divorce is staying in a marriage that is destroying your happiness.

3. Be grateful that you woke up this morning with the ability to breathe and face the day. As long as you are still breathing, you have the ability to change your life.

4. Be grateful if you live in a country where you are allowed to be divorced.

5. Be grateful if you are a woman who doesn't fear death as a punishment for leaving her husband. Be courageous if otherwise.

6. If you are seventy years old, and you fear meeting another mate, be grateful that you aren't one hundred years old and looking for another mate.

7. If you will lose all of your money in the divorce, be grateful that you know how to make more money.

> *"What does not kill us makes us stronger."*
> *Frederich Nietzsche*

Choosing an attitude of gratitude is an important tool to help you to be a champion instead of a victim. We don't choose to be victimized, but we do choose to act like victims.

Right now, you have the opportunity to be grateful for the fact that you have just exposed yourself to a wealth of positive concepts. Be grateful that you have the ability to read, since eleven percent of born and bred North Americans cannot read or write.

Choosing to be grateful is choosing to be good to yourself. Anytime you choose gratitude over self-pity, you are choosing a positive, instead of a negative, thought stream.

Choosing to place positive energy in your life is choosing to construct your life. Choosing negative energy is choosing self-destruction.

CONCLUSION

The concept of choosing positive over negative applies to all of the keys. Each key has the opposite choice available. You can choose to be positive or negative, constructive or destructive. **Your life is yours to build, and it is yours to destroy. Taking charge of "how you think" is taking charge of your life.**

> *"The happiness of your life depends on the quality of your thoughts; therefore, guard accordingly and take care that you entertain no notions unsuitable to virtue and reasonable nature."*
>
> **Marcus Antonius**

Be responsible and accountable for your thoughts and your actions, as every action starts out as a thought.

None of us lives in a bubble. Our thoughts are a form of energy, and they have an effect on those around us. Remember that any temper tantrum, gossip session, or pity party will do harm to anyone whom you touch with that negative energy. By being aware of how your actions affect others, you will have more control over your choice of actions. You can yell at the girl in the drive-through window and wreck her day, or you can smile and pay her a nice compliment. Which choice do you think will make **her** feel better? Which choice do you think will make **you** feel better? Which will make the world better?

Of course, if the girl in the drive through window was a master of all of the keys, she would not be offended by a buffoon who needs to yell at her. Unfortunately, very few people are practitioners of higher thought. The chances are that the girl in the window is a regular human being with a regular skill set. How you choose to treat her will almost certainly have an effect on her. Even if by chance your actions do not affect her, your actions will still affect you. Choosing to be positive is choosing to be good to yourself. If you have learned to love and accept yourself, you will then have the strength to treat yourself well.

> **Instead of only walking the paths that will bring more toys into your garage, spend some time on the paths that will bring more joy into your life. It's not the toys; it's the joy that we are really striving for.**

> *Think positive, think free;*
> *Live positive, Live free.*
> *- Mark Edward Meincke*

More inspiration

> *"Courage is realizing you're afraid and still acting."*
>
> *Rudi Guiliani*

> *"A bit of advice given to a young Native American at the time of his initiation: 'As you go the way of life, you will see a great chasm. Jump. It is not as wide as you think.'"*
>
> *Joseph Campbell*

> *"There came a time when the risk to remain tight in the bud was more painful than the risk it took to blossom."*
>
> *Anais Nin*

> *"If we didn't live venturously, plucking the wild goat by the beard, and trembling over precipices, we should never be depressed, I've no doubt, but already should be faded, fatalistic and aged."*
>
> *Virginia Woolf*

> *"The meaning I picked, the one that changed my life: Overcome fear, behold wonder."*
>
> *Richard Bach*

"Have courage for the great sorrows of life and patience for the small ones, and when you have laboriously accomplished your daily task, go to sleep in peace. God is awake."

Victor Hugo

"It takes a lot of courage to release the familiar and seemingly secure, to embrace the new. There is more security in the adventurous and exciting, for in movement there is life, and in change there is power."

Alan Cohen

"This is courage in a man: to bear unflinchingly what heaven sends."

Euripedes

"The man who makes no mistakes does not usually make anything."

Bishop W.C. Magee

"Every time you meet a situation, though you think at the time it is an impossibility and you go through the tortures of the damned, once you have met it and lived through it, you find that forever after you are freer than you were before."

Eleanor Roosevelt

"Cowards die many times before their deaths; the valiant never taste of death but once."

William Shakespeare

"One's real life is often the life that one does not lead."

Oscar Wilde

"Obstacles are those frightful things you see when you take your eyes off your goal."

Henry Ford

"Twenty years from now you will be more disappointed by the things you didn't do than by the ones you did do. So throw off the bowlines. Sail away from the safe harbor. Catch the trade winds in your sails. Explore. Dream. Discover."

Mark Twain

*"We never know how high we are Till we are called to rise;
And then, if we are true to plan, Our statures touch the skies."*

Emily Dickinson

"To dare is to lose one's footing momentarily. Not to dare is to lose oneself."

Soren Kierkegaard

"What would you attempt to do if you knew you could not fail?"
                              Marianne Williamson

"One doesn't discover new lands without consenting to lose sight of the shore for a very long time."
                              Andre Gide

"Ultimately we know deeply that the other side of every fear is a freedom."
                              Marilyn Ferguson

"Plunge boldly into the thick of life!"
                              Goethe

"Confidence, like art, never comes from having all the answers; it comes from being open to all the questions."
                              Earl Gray Stevens

"What worries you, masters you."
                              Haddon W. Robinson

"One must think like a hero merely to behave like a decent human being."
                              May Barton

About the Author

Mark Meincke is known as a profoundly insightful problem solver with an almost childlike curiosity about how things work & why they are how they are.

His natural talents enable him to reverse engineer results in order to indentify the key factors that caused them.

Mr. Meincke is highly regarded as an authority on achievement psychology, and is widely recognized as a dynamic, engaging speaker.